"Caleb Kaltenbach lets us know that even if today looks bleak, our future is right with God. God never changes and in no way will abandon us, yet he chooses to transform us and revolutionizes his world through us. Thank you, Caleb, for reminding us that our good God is here now and is going to be here tomorrow."

—KYLE IDLEMAN, best-selling author of *Not a Fan* and *Grace Is Greater*

"We have no idea how much rises and falls on our ability to love people. *God of Tomorrow* gives us perspective to love others well, no matter what—not only because everyone matters to God but also because we matter. And love is the only path to freedom."

—KRISTEN IVY, executive director of messaging at Orange
and founder of the Phase Project

"Jesus told us to love our neighbors, because He knew that love changes everything. If you want to be challenged to love, invest in, and serve your neighbor, then I can't recommend *God of Tomorrow* more highly."

—REGGIE JOINER, founder and CEO of Orange

"In an age when most voices seem extreme and debate is highly polarized, Caleb brings a needed sane, faithful perspective. He will show you how to keep your heart and mind engaged in a culture that you might not like but still need to love."

—CAREY NIEUWHOF, founding pastor of Connexus Church
and author of *Didn't See It Coming*

"More than anything else, what our chaotic and complicated world needs is hope. Caleb Kaltenbach reminds us that Jesus is the only place where hope is found and encourages us to live so that others might see hope within us."

—RUSSELL MOORE, president of the Ethics and Religious Liberty
Commission of the Southern Baptist Convention

"In *God of Tomorrow,* Caleb Kaltenbach couples brilliant insight with compassion. He powerfully demonstrates how we can exchange fear for faith and invite others into hope for the future. This well-written book is an essential guide for navigating the changes of life and culture with grace and truth."

—Jud Wilhite, senior pastor of Central Church
and author of *Pursued*

"The best thing about our God is that he's the same yesterday, today, and tomorrow. This work, shaped by Caleb's unique life experience and perspective, is an important conversation for 'such a time as this.' Thanks, Caleb, for taking the deep dive into hard conversations!"

—Tyler Reagin, president of Catalyst

"Rather than any words we say, it's how we treat people that communicates God's love. *God of Tomorrow* will help you show people the love of God."

—Carlos Whittaker, author of *Kill the Spider*

"I love Caleb's disarming style of delivering tough, enduring truths. He is an authentic voice for this generation."

—Dennis Rainey, cofounder of FamilyLife, a Cru ministry

"In a growingly divisive world, the church is at a crossroads. Caleb's work provides a powerful and hopeful way forward that every Christian needs! In fact, the future influence of the church might just depend on whether or not we choose to apply the road map provided by *God of Tomorrow*."

—Clay Scroggins, lead pastor of North Point Community Church
and author of *How to Lead When You're Not in Charge*

"Kaltenbach is a voice of hope for Christians struggling to remain at ease despite the uncertainties of today. I affirm his gracious reminder to Christians that the future is relentlessly and eternally hopeful, regardless of political and social upheaval. *God of Tomorrow* propels Christ followers to trust in God, who never changes and never ceases to watch over his people."

—Barry H. Corey, president of Biola University and author
of *Love Kindness*

"Hurting people don't need clever advice or another self-help book—they need the gospel! They're desperate to know the God who cares, is in control, and has a plan for their lives. In *God of Tomorrow,* my friend Caleb gives us tools so we can point to the Savior who gives us a future and offers hope."

—Dr. Jack Graham, pastor of Prestonwood Baptist Church

"For people of faith, tomorrow can be confusing when colored by the changing world we live in today. I'm thankful that Caleb Kaltenbach has given us another must-read book that practically and biblically helps us navigate the chaos of today and restores genuine hope for tomorrow."

—Gene Appel, senior pastor of Eastside Christian Church

"How do we as imperfect people offer hope to a broken world? Caleb urges us to look beyond ourselves. If we focus on God's power and plan of redemption, we'll discover renewed courage to share hope."

—Mike Foster, author of *People of the Second Chance*

"Combining solid biblical content with a pastoral heart that engages the cultural issues of the day, Caleb provides hope and encouragement for followers of Jesus amid the challenges our culture presents to faithfully living out biblical convictions. This is a calm and well-reasoned voice that is much needed today.

—Scott B. Rae, Ph.D, dean of faculty and professor of
Christian ethics at Talbot School of Theology, Biola University

"The world is broken and people are hurting. Though society doesn't always offer healthy solutions, Jesus followers have what's needed. In *God of Tomorrow,* my friend Caleb reminds us that God's promise to redeem empowers us to be people of joy with a message of hope."

—Gabe Lyons, founder of Q Ideas and author of *Good Faith*

"I don't know many people who've been through as much uncertainty and change as my friend Caleb. If your tomorrow looks similar, you need to devour this book."

—Ashley Wooldridge, senior pastor of Christ's Church of the Valley

"Caleb Kaltenbach has a unique perspective on culture and faith. From the roots of his story in *Messy Grace,* he has forged a foothold in both worlds that enables him to embrace reality without abandoning hope. If you struggle with getting though the day after reading the headlines, then *God of Tomorrow* is a must-read."

> —LANE JONES, executive director of multisite ministry at North
> Point Ministries

"*God of Tomorrow* speaks life and hope into this world by reminding us who we follow and who holds our future. This is a must-read for any person who's ever thought, *Everything seems to be getting worse!*"

> —RUSTY GEORGE, lead pastor of Real Life Church and author
> of *When You, Then God* and *Better Together*

"Caleb Kaltenbach is an exceptional storyteller with a passion to point others back to the gospel of Jesus Christ. This book is much needed in a society that needs to know there is hope for the future."

> —JASON ROMANO, former ESPN producer and author
> of *Live to Forgive*

"With wise insight and pastoral skill, Caleb constantly lifts our gaze from the difficulty and toxicity of frightening headlines, cultural chaos, and even personal trials to the One who rules and loves."

> —JARED C. WILSON, director of content strategy at Midwestern
> Baptist Theological Seminary and author of *Supernatural
> Power for Everyday People*

"As Christians our priority should be clear: share Jesus by relentlessly loving people, no matter what. This should happen more often, but too many of us fight against or fear society. In *God of Tomorrow,* my friend Caleb helps us discover courage to share hope with people who so desperately need it."

> —DR. TIM HARLOW, senior pastor of Parkview Christian Church
> and author of *Life on Mission*

"In this winsomely unique book, anchored in the antique truth of Scripture, my friend Caleb Kaltenbach reminds us that God is not popping Tums over tomorrow. He is in control, so we need not fear. We can actually rejoice. What a refreshing book!"

> —BRYAN LORITTS, lead pastor of Abundant Life Christian Fellowship
> and author of *Saving the Saved*

GOD
OF
TOMORROW

HOW TO OVERCOME
THE FEARS OF TODAY AND
RENEW YOUR HOPE
FOR THE FUTURE

CALEB KALTENBACH

AUTHOR OF *MESSY GRACE*

WATERBROOK

All Scripture quotations, unless otherwise indicated, are taken from the Holy Bible, New International Version®, NIV®. Copyright © 1973, 1978, 1984, 2011 by Biblica Inc.® Used by permission. All rights reserved worldwide. Scripture quotations marked (ESV) are taken from the Holy Bible, English Standard Version, ESV® Text Edition® (2016), copyright © 2001 by Crossway Bibles, a publishing ministry of Good News Publishers. All rights reserved. Scripture quotations marked (NCV) are taken from the New Century Version®. Copyright © 2005 by Thomas Nelson Inc. Used by permission. All rights reserved. Scripture quotations marked (NLT) are taken from the Holy Bible, New Living Translation, copyright © 1996, 2004, 2007, 2013, 2015 by Tyndale House Foundation. Used by permission of Tyndale House Publishers Inc., Carol Stream, Illinois 60188. All rights reserved.

Italics in Scripture quotations reflect the author's added emphasis.

Details in some anecdotes and stories have been changed to protect the identities of the persons involved.

Trade Paperback ISBN 978-0-7352-8998-7
eBook ISBN 978-0-7352-8999-4

Copyright © 2018 by Caleb W. Kaltenbach

Cover design by Kristopher K. Orr; cover image by Alin Suciu, 500px

Published in the United States by WaterBrook, an imprint of the Crown Publishing Group, a division of Penguin Random House LLC, New York.

WATERBROOK® and its deer colophon are registered trademarks of Penguin Random House LLC.

Library of Congress Cataloging-in-Publication Data
Names: Kaltenbach, Caleb, author.
Title: God of tomorrow : how to overcome the fears of today and renew your hope for the future / Caleb W. Kaltenbach.
Description: First Edition. | Colorado Springs : WaterBrook, 2018. | Includes bibliographical references.
Identifiers: LCCN 2017041015 | ISBN 9780735289987 (pbk.) | ISBN 9780735289994 (electronic)
Subjects: LCSH: Trust in God—Christianity. | Christianity and culture.
Classification: LCC BV4637 .K354 2018 | DDC 261—dc23
LC record available at https://lccn.loc.gov/2017041015

Printed in the United States of America
2018—First Edition

10 9 8 7 6 5 4 3 2 1

SPECIAL SALES
Most WaterBrook books are available at special quantity discounts when purchased in bulk by corporations, organizations, and special-interest groups. Custom imprinting or excerpting can also be done to fit special needs. For information, please e-mail specialmarketscms@penguin randomhouse.com or call 1-800-603-7051.

To Mike Foster, Mark Moore, Jud Wilhite, and Tim Winters—

*You were among the first to really know me. Because of you,
I believe that tomorrow is never devoid of hope. Thank you.*

Contents

WE DON'T KNOW
WHAT TOMORROW
HOLDS, BUT WE
KNOW WHO
HOLDS
TOMORROW.

1

Punched by Tomorrow

It was midmorning on Friday, June 26, 2015, and I was getting ready for the final day of a Christian leadership conference I was attending. I had spent a long week in Cincinnati with friends and ministry colleagues. The days had been filled with meetings and speaking opportunities about my then-upcoming book *Messy Grace,* in which I tell my story of growing up with both parents in same-sex relationships, becoming a follower of Jesus, and learning how to relate to both the LGBTQ community and the Christian community. I was looking forward to a less busy weekend and returning to California to be with my wife and kids.

Then the text alert on my phone went off. I was puzzled by the message. A friend had merely sent this line: "God help us." I wasn't sure what his text meant but figured maybe it was some awkward spiritual encouragement.

Remembering I wanted to be on time for the morning's final main session, I set the phone down, turned the volume off, and finished packing and getting ready. Nearly ready to walk out the door with my suitcase, I picked up my wallet and phone. I noticed my phone was displaying text message after text message. Some of them read as follows:

"What are you going to preach on now?"

"God is still in control."

"You need to celebrate with people on Sunday!"

"This is a chance for you to stand up for what's right."

There were many other texts, but one let me know exactly what had happened. A pastor friend texted me, "Bro, I sure wish your book was available now." The Supreme Court had been expected to announce its decision on *Obergefell v. Hodges* (marriage equality). No doubt it had been announced that the court had ruled in favor of same-sex marriage, and thus the wave of text after text.

Just as I was about to check the news, I got a call on my cell phone. It was a number from my home area code, so I answered—I thought it could be my wife or kids using somebody else's phone. In a glimpse of what was to come this weekend, the call was from a journalist with a Southern California newspaper. "Reverend Kaltenbach, what is your reaction to the Supreme Court ruling?"

I didn't answer at first. It took me a couple of moments. I hadn't even seen a news broadcast, read an article, or listened to an interview since the court announcement. The wheels in my mind were still spinning. My mom, her partner (Vera), and my dad had talked about this day for years. They couldn't wait to celebrate a day like this. But certainly not everyone felt the same. During my week in Cincinnati, I'd had a few conversations with pastors and leaders about the upcoming ruling on marriage equality. Some asked if I believed the Supreme Court would rule in favor of keeping marriage between one man and one woman. My answer to them was simple: "Nope." This response hadn't been greeted with universal joy.

As quickly as I could, I ended the call with the journalist, turned off my phone, and headed out of the hotel room to put my luggage in my car. Shortly afterward, as I walked out of the parking garage, I saw that the change in society had already reached downtown Cincinnati. The streets had been lined with rainbow flags during the week, but now there were more. A gay pride parade had been scheduled for downtown later that weekend, but with the ruling now public, the celebration had started early. People were dancing on the sidewalks, cheering, hugging, high-fiving, and shouting, "Victory! Victory!" Loud celebratory music was pumping from cars, and a few people were running through the streets. Meanwhile, a couple of people were waving homemade signs of protest on street corners.

When I walked into the convention center, the doors to the main hall opened and people began walking out as I was walking in. Some pastors had their heads down; some were obviously angry; some were expressing their happiness that there was equality in marriage. A variety of emotions filled the crowd leaving the session.

One new acquaintance came up to me as he exited the main session. Earlier in the week, he had been in a workshop I had taught on the church and the LGBTQ community. I remembered that he'd had a series of questions after I taught the workshop. Today he shook my hand and said, "Well, thank you for trying." What in the world did that even mean? His next comment puzzled me even more: "I don't know what tomorrow holds."

Then he walked away without even giving me a chance to respond. I didn't know his name, but I knew that he and a lot of people were in a tailspin on this day. Probably most Christians who are conservative or evangelical or who identify as such saw this as a day when everything in America changed. I can understand that (especially from a political standpoint), but for me everything had changed a while ago. Actually, even before I became a Christian as a teenager, I knew that a major shift in society was taking place. Still, my acquaintance's fearful words bothered me: *I don't know what tomorrow holds.*

This book, unlike my last book, is *not* primarily about some Christian attitudes toward people who identify as LGBTQ. The book you're about to read examines a much wider range of issues we face. More importantly, it goes to the heart of what we believe about God, ourselves, and the future.

And let's be honest: it's not just a Supreme Court decision that some evangelical and conservative Christian leaders fear. It's not just a conservative takeover of the government that some progressive Christians worry about. Political, social, cultural, economic, and relational fears across a broad spectrum drive our emotions and frame our outlooks. I've been trying to figure out why the concept of *tomorrow* can be so frightening. I think it's the unknown that drives our fear.

TOMORROW CAN BE A CREEPER

For many people, the concept of *tomorrow* is uncertain, alarming, and even terrifying. I mean, tomorrow is not something you can count on, right? It can be full of surprises. Tomorrow almost seems as if it has multiple personalities; sometimes it brings us good news and other times not-so-good news.

Many nights over the course of my life, I have gone to bed not knowing all the wonderful things tomorrow would bring. My tomorrows have given me the first days of new school years, new friends, an invitation to a high school Bible study that would teach me about Jesus, graduations, an exciting job at a church in Southern California, an introduction to the gorgeous woman who would become my wife, the births of my kids, new adventures, and so on. Even when I have my down periods, I have to admit there have been many good days in my life.

But there have also been many tomorrows that have negatively affected the course of my life. One time when I was two years old, I didn't understand that the next day my parents would decide to divorce. I had no idea as I went to bed one night in December 1996 that I'd wake up to the news that my cousin had been killed in a horrible accident. Not long ago, the next day caught me by surprise when I heard that my wife's father had had an aortic dissection and aneurysm. I could go on, but you understand that my tomorrows have been filled with lows as well as highs. So have yours.

And not only do we see uncertainty in tomorrow, but the leaders and writers of the Bible saw it too. Verses such as the following remind us of tomorrow's ambiguity:

> Do not boast about tomorrow,
>   for you do not know what a day may bring. (Proverbs 27:1)

> When life is good, enjoy it.
>   But when life is hard, remember:
> God gives good times and hard times,
>   and no one knows what tomorrow will bring. (Ecclesiastes
>   7:14, NCV)

> Come now, you who say, "Today or tomorrow we will go into
> such and such a town and spend a year there and trade and make
> a profit"—yet you do not know what tomorrow will bring. (James
> 4:13–14, ESV)

The events of tomorrow were unpredictable for the people in the Bible:

- Abraham would leave his home for an unknown land far away.
- Sarah would laugh at the mere thought of pregnancy.
- Moses would kill an Egyptian, and his life would never be the same.
- Deborah would be named the leader of her people.

- Samson's girlfriend would betray him, and he would be captured.
- David would have an affair and unleash a chaotic chain of events.
- Elijah would run from a queen after watching God defeat his enemies.
- Esther would muster the courage to expose Haman's evil.
- A woman by a well would meet the God who created her.
- John the Baptist would be thrown into prison.
- Peter would deny Jesus three times.
- Mary Magdalene and the disciples would see the risen Christ.
- An Ethiopian eunuch would hear about the gospel.

All these people were just like you, me, and everyone else who is alive on this planet right now. We're all individuals stuck in the arena of time who experience the progression of life through uncertain days.

The future relentlessly engages us, whether we want it to or not.

Whatever tomorrow brings, the fact that it will deliver something good or bad remains inevitable. The future relentlessly engages us, whether we want it to or not. Today and its status quo might seem solid enough, but as William Shakespeare said, tomorrow is always creeping up on us.

To-morrow, and to-morrow, and to-morrow,
  Creeps in this petty pace from day to day,
  To the last syllable of recorded time.[1]

I don't know if anybody has noticed this before, but Bill has a way with words. And he's right about tomorrow's persistence.

All of us have to face the reality of tomorrow and the changes it will bring. When we look at the world and see the changes that have occurred and imagine the ones that might happen, fear may enter our souls like cold iron.

WHY TOMORROW MIGHT CAUSE FEAR

Let me make it clear that this book is not about our personal fears for tomorrow, though we have plenty of them—and they are important. You may be worried about the stability of your job, a loved one's health, supporting a friend during her crisis, how to fix your marriage, or many more personal or family problems. I know these life situations weigh heavily on your heart, as they weigh on mine, too. In this book, however, we're focusing more on the large-scale social changes that affect us all. The encouragement this book brings can apply easily to your personal problems, and I hope you'll take it to heart. What I'm particularly trying to address is the widespread issue I see in Christians of all political and theological persuasions who fear tomorrow because of what they see transpiring in society. I don't believe God wants us to have a toxic fear of the future or to get stuck in anxiety (even though the fear of what's happening in society is common and serious).

And in a sense these changes in society *are* personal. Sooner or later, many of them will invade our lives and relationships. They'll affect us individually by altering our moods or influencing us in more direct and tangible ways.

Maybe some of us have coworkers of a different ethnicity who have a dissimilar perspective on society and political beliefs than others do.

When they encounter people who don't understand their viewpoint, they may think, *I bet they've never been attacked just because of the color of their skin. I'm sure they haven't walked into a clothing store and had to deal with the salespeople eyeing them the whole time. I wonder if they've ever gone into an elevator and noticed the woman in the back grasping her purse tighter just because they got on the elevator.* As we hear our friends talk, we can't help but wonder if some of us are really *that* unaware of the privilege and resources we may have been afforded in childhood.

Or it could be that we begin our day by watching the news and reading articles that reflect the polarization of politics. Later on during the day, we have lunch with a friend who voted for the "other candidate." A voting record hasn't ever been a conversation stopper for us before, but now it seems that our friend becomes more incensed as our talk gravitates toward politics. It's then that we realize how much the enormous gap between political parties has removed the potential for thoughtful dialogue with this friend. Perhaps later that night, as we watch the news channel we agree with, our emotions lean toward dismay as we consider the future of religious freedom, presidential administrations, the implications of various bills Congress might pass, social unrest, and so on.

Those examples of social change are just a start. Unfortunately, a segment in our society has a problem with our culture becoming more multiethnic. Some don't think of racism as a huge problem in America, despite acts of violence and the continual cries of our people. We argue about immigration, the ethics of immigration reform, and the importance of loving refugees, yet somehow we forget that these discussions are more than political platforms; they're about actual people with families, needs, and stories. As the months go on, some see our society drifting further from Judeo-Christian values, while there's an increase in broken families and teen suicides that reveals society's lack of concern for hurting people. There are a few who seek to put restrictions on some individuals' expressions of faith. Today, people live in fear of terrorists and don't even consider the atrocities committed by some governments and regimes around the world. Political leaders in a few states would count the legalization of marijuana as a victory, but have they really counted the cost of such a move? More than ever, we see a loss of civility in public discourse, the devaluing of honest conversation amid disagreements, and vile social media posts. Our prison population is increasing, shootings are becoming all too familiar, natural resources are under attack, a few politicians on both sides of the aisle are becoming more extreme, and the list could go on and on. At the root of it, for me, is that a growing number of people see a relationship with Jesus as irrelevant.

Wherever you are in your political ideology, theological convictions, and moral beliefs, I'm sure we can agree that today's world isn't the world we grew up in, no matter when or where we grew up. Society has changed. Society will change. And change can be unsettling.

SOCIETY—ALWAYS CHANGING, ALWAYS THE SAME

Change. That word can strike fear into the heart of your average organized, systematic, A-type personality. For some people, the word *change* brings other words with it, such as *upheaval, hurt, loss, move, shift,* and similar terms that indicate difficult life transitions.

For others, change is more positive. It can represent newness, progress, innovative ideas, positive emotions, and more. People who like change probably work (or want to work) in an environment where their job description and tasks shift depending on the season.

The 2008 presidential election showed us the influence of this word.

Senator Barack Obama's one-word slogans "Hope" and "Change" left a memorable impression on people's minds. His supporters ate up the idea of the change he would provide. Senator John McCain's supporters, however, automatically used the word *change* to refer to a negative change they feared an Obama administration would bring to the country.

A few years later, when Donald Trump ascended to the presidency, many on both sides of the political aisle decried the changes they saw coming from the White House.

Whatever our personality types, we all respond differently to change in society. The very nature of change forces a reorganization of our lives. As a result, our view of change is often dramatic, whether dramatically optimistic or dramatically worried.

Regardless, we've got to get used to change.

Over the years, I've heard fellow pastors and Christians from all backgrounds lament, "Society is changing" or "Society is getting worse" (however that particular person defines *worse*). Well, of course society is changing! Society always changes. Society is directly affected by the changing world around it, with changes in technology, the global political climate, trends, media, generational priorities, ethnic makeup, and more. Society can and does change for the better or the worse—it depends on how a particular society is structured and what values are woven within the fabric of the culture.

Society always changes . . . but it also stays the same.

Here's what I mean: While society is always shifting, the core foundational issues we struggle with as a society are not new. Fundamentally, there is nothing any present-day society is processing that societies of the past did not work through.

Every trend or event that has occurred in our day is based on a more fundamental human issue that Jesus, Paul, Peter, and other biblical leaders had to address in a different way. Do me a favor before moving to the next chapter: read or review the Old Testament book of Ecclesiastes. You'll quickly discover that even Old Testament leaders had to deal with similar controversies and clashing ideas.

If that doesn't help you feel better, how about the fact that Jesus, Peter, and other individuals in the Bible had the same societal issues we do in our country, *only worse*? Our society has some major moral and ethical gaps, but we don't face the degree of danger that was prevalent in the first century. While their society and ours have both experienced crumbling marriages, human trafficking, slavery, and so on, the way the early Christians experienced such societal movements was harsher and resulted in the deaths of many Christians.

There is nothing any present-day society is processing that societies of the past did not work through.

In the first century, a majority of Christians lived in the Roman Empire, which was led by a succession of dictators, some of whom were so narcissistic that they believed they were divine. (We'll get into that sorry situation more later.) Meanwhile, the superstition of other religions inside the empire was unbelievable. The ethics and values that Christians held contrasted starkly to those of the Greco-Roman world. This frequently led to misunderstanding, slander, persecution, exile, and, as I just mentioned, death for Christians.

Now, what was it you posted on social media that you thought was an outrage?

There's no comparison between society for first-century Christians, societies in the Old Testament era, and our American society. The closest similarity in today's world might be the society of some countries in the Middle East and the cultural norms Christians have to struggle through.

Yet when Jesus, Peter, and Paul interacted with people far from God, they didn't get mad at them. They had strong biblical beliefs and strong friendships with various people, even those far from God. All I'm suggesting is that we can and should do the same.

WAYS TO INTERACT WITH SOCIETY

Even though the concerns in our society may not be as new or extreme as we have been assuming, they are present. God put us here in this generation and expects us to represent him faithfully wherever we are. So, what should we do with our anxieties regarding the future? How should we approach a society that frequently changes in ways we don't appreciate?

Option A: Aggressively Fight a Broken Society

Just so you know, I completely understand that we all have different views when it comes to the intersection of Christianity and the trends of society. For instance, some of us feel as though we are in a battle with society because of our faith and, as such, need to stand up for what's right. We reason that if we don't speak up, who will?

If that describes your attitude, let me say that I can relate. As a matter of fact, within the pages of this book, you'll find a lot of support for the concept of boldness. I would even go so far as to say that if we are Christians, we have no choice but to speak up boldly against the wrongs we see. If you think about it, that's probably why Jesus called us to be salt and light (Matthew 5:13–16). The Bible is filled with examples of God sending his people to not only speak firmly but also stand in opposition to the wrong and injustice in the world.

Yet while many Christians have taken brave stands against the marginalization of people, harmful social programs, and the like, there are also examples of Christians who, in their efforts to stand up for truth, have actually hurt society. They've at least been perceived as being too aggressive (some are) and lacking empathy for those with opposing views (many do).

Combativeness without compassion is always going to be counterproductive.

Anytime we find ourselves despising or putting down a community, it really means that we have a problem with people, because communities are made up of people. Whether you disagree with and disdain the NRA Second Amendment rights crowd, the scholarly academic crowd, Muslims in your city, Hollywood, the GOP or the DNC, the corporation your spouse works for, illegal immigrants, conservative Christians, citizens of a certain country, the millennial generation, or any other community, any hateful feelings you may have toward these people are opposite of the feelings God has for them. Combativeness without compassion is always going to be counterproductive.

Option B: Surrender and Fully Hop On Board with Society

In contrast to the combative Christians, some of us are jaded from adverse attitudes of other people, so we decide that it's better never to bring up controversial social issues. It might be that you've seen your fair share of people turned off by the church because of how Christians have treated them, so you've committed to acting differently. You identify with verses that talk about God's love and you emphasize those verses without mentioning any of the ones that conflict with society's values. It's not that you don't love God and the Bible, but more than likely you've concluded that you'll make a greater impression by staying silent on lightning-rod issues. Along those same lines, someone you love might have adopted a belief that was more aligned with a popular trend in society than with God's words. For you, it's been easier to support society's "latest and greatest" than to do anything else. If so, I definitely get where you're coming from (I find myself there sometimes), but that just isn't a beneficial approach. Silence about people's mistakes in the face of their pain doesn't help them—it hurts them.

Basing our values on our favorite celebrity, political leader, author, good friend, or simply the opinion of the majority in the moment assures disappointment. What do we do when society changes again or the person we admire shifts his or her opinion and differs with us on an important issue?

Aligning our views with society's latest slant results in the constant shifting of our views. Because society is always in flux and its values are always changing, it's impossible to have a consistent worldview when we're eager to go along with society. In a few chapters, we'll discuss the necessity of adjusting how we present truth to society, but let me emphasize right now that we should never change our orthodox beliefs to line up with a culture that is constantly changing. Those who measure their convictions against an ever-shifting society will always be adjusting their beliefs. Very rarely does society remain in one place.

As you can see, this approach holds many problems. We need another way.

Option C: Invest in Society with Empathy and Conviction

As opposed to words such as *fight* and *surrender,* the word *invest* paints a picture of people giving of themselves to improve the world around them. It means that you and I don't just write blogs or talk boldly *about* cultural problems; we sacrifice and invest *in* the lives of others in society. For me, *invest* is another way of saying the word *engage.* Engagement encompasses learning about a certain context or group of people to better understand them. I believe we should invest in and engage people around us; we should be the first ones to initiate a relationship and not wait on others. Developing relationships with people not like us or people who might intimidate us is so necessary. Our differences with people should drive us *to* them, not *from* them.

If you hadn't guessed yet, option C is the view we'll explore in this book. I believe it's the option that makes the most sense.

Our differences with people should drive us *to* them, not *from* them.

When we're afraid of what tomorrow holds for society and respond by fighting against people, surrendering to misguided ideas, or simply showing indifference to growing causes around the world, we're choosing to mistreat and devalue others. Not only is dismissing people never a valid option, but it isn't pleasing to God. Don't go in that direction. Make the better choice.

I hope that by the end of this book you'll see society differently and be fully convinced that any Jesus follower who makes a godly investment in people will make a difference in the world.

Just Your Average, Everyday World Changers

Two of my favorite people in the whole world are John and Marla. I'm not certain whether they have ever spoken at a conference, written a book, penned an article, blogged, or been guests on a podcast, but I can assure you that you would be inspired if you met them.

I got to meet them when my family and I lived in the Dallas–Fort Worth area. I was pastoring a church near Plano that had a lot of promise, but the congregation didn't reflect the demographics of families living around the church. The congregation's average age was older and its makeup mostly Caucasian among a community that was becoming more multiethnic. So a couple of months after I came on staff, I challenged the small groups in the church to engage in some kind of outreach to their immediate community.

Many groups did some fantastic outreaches, but John and Marla's group was the most mesmerizing to me. This couple's daughter taught in a local public high school and had told them about a young student who had just had a baby. She shared how much this girl loved school but was struggling to balance her roles as a young mother and a high school student. She was losing her fight to complete her education, and that broke their hearts. Even more sobering was the knowledge that without her getting a diploma, the future for this young family would look even bleaker.

John and Marla could have looked down on a girl who had irresponsibly engaged in sex before marriage. They could have ignored the hard times she was going through with her baby. But instead they saw a chance to make a difference, and they decided to do something for her and for similar young moms and their infants.

Within a couple of weeks, the small group hosted a baby shower for teen moms in the area. The idea was simple: provide a safe harbor where these girls could come together and have some fun and find encouragement and love. The group decorated the lobby of the church, gathered other volunteers, and had some of the best Texas barbecue catered. They passed out much-needed gifts of baby gear. While they had only a few moms attend this first event, these moms were forever changed because of the love they saw from this group of people.

Not long after that baby shower, John and Marla asked me if they could do this kind of event regularly. "By all means!" I responded. Just watching their excitement and passion for God and people inspired me. I couldn't wait to see how God would use this idea.

Over the next months, word spread and the events grew. The first Tuesday of each month became a time the girls planned for and told others about. In addition to a baby shower once a year (many of the girls had never had one), they did games, karaoke, crafts, and other fun things teens enjoy. As the number of volunteers grew, so did the number of ideas for how to make these teen moms and their extended families feel special. John and Marla even got volunteers to play basketball with the babies' fathers at each event.

As people volunteered to help, some would ask questions such as, "Shouldn't we talk to these young ladies about life so they don't get pregnant again?" I'm sure the question was well intended, but it also showed a lack of understanding and empathy.

I loved how John answered one such question. As I listened in, he said, "As we get to know these young ladies, we have opportunities to talk to them about faith and life. But we have to remember they have already had their babies; the question now is, how are we going to respond? They chose life and we should celebrate their decision by coming alongside and loving them. Many of the girls have already faced rejection, in some cases from their own church. A decision to come to our church, where they could be judged again, is scary. But because they realized they needed help, they attended our church. And isn't that what we're here for—to help and love them?"

I was thrilled to see someone respond to a vulnerable segment of our community with such empathy and conviction. We need more of these ideas to engage our neighborhoods, cities, and society.

Today, that ministry is called Blessing Teen Parents. They have been helping teen moms since 2010. Each year, the number of moms attending their monthly events has grown. Many of these moms end up asking questions about faith, trusting Jesus, and even attending church. John and Marla, along with their amazing volunteers, have shown teen moms in their area the importance of staying in school, how to love their kids, and the power of acceptance, and they have even provided scholarships for college.

They're not fretting about the future; they're influencing it. They're not bemoaning a trend; they're engaging those who are part of the trend. They're just your average, everyday world changers!

FREE FROM FEAR, FREE TO LOVE

Now let me go back to where I started this chapter. The interaction with my new acquaintance in Cincinnati—the one who said he didn't know what tomorrow holds—plagued me. It wasn't so much his words in the moment but the mind-set lying behind his words that bothered me. And I know he's not the only one to have such a mind-set. Far from it. For many Christians (myself sometimes included), when something happens in society that we consider to be wrong or unjust, we can feel a sense of doom and hopelessness. It paralyzes us. It may even bring out the worst in us.

I'm not saying we shouldn't express grief or disappointment when our society heads in directions we disagree with, whether those directions are labeled *liberal* or *conservative* or something else. We should. Everyone has fears. If you've had any leadership responsibilities that included making tough decisions, you'll agree with what I've heard many Christian leaders say: "Fear is a constant companion in leadership." However, I'd like to amend that statement by saying, "Fear is a constant companion in life." However, we shouldn't let fear control us. We're in trouble when toxic fear begins to dictate our thinking and actions. I've seen this toxic fear in so many people, including my Cincinnati acquaintance.

If I could have that encounter again, I'd speak up before my friend walked away. I'd resurrect a phrase that's been used in some form by many Christian leaders: "We don't know what tomorrow holds, but we know who holds tomorrow." My Cincinnati friend and all the rest of us need to have a robust trust that God is still in control, has a plan, and is working out his plan in the midst of what's happening today and what's coming tomorrow. Such faith in God will calm some of our fears—and that's great, right? But the faith we'll be discussing in this book can do more than just calm our fears. By the time you turn the final page of the book, I want you to have faith that focuses on the mission God has given you as his representative in the world. Because how you view tomorrow affects how you live today.

Let me give you a preview of the message I'm going to be repeating and elaborating on throughout the course of this book. It's a simple idea but nonetheless one we can easily forget in the heat of society's tensions. We have to burn this idea into our very souls. I believe that this truth is what Jesus would have you remember, as opposed to regretting the past and fearing the present or future.

The God of Tomorrow Principle

Since tomorrow belongs to God, we can graciously offer hope to people today.

I'm going to discuss each of the key parts of the God of Tomorrow principle in the chapters of this book. If we really think deeper about the elements of this axiom, we can charge tomorrow with hope instead of being dragged into it kicking and screaming. This principle will help us to better invest in society by engaging people, no matter who they are, where they're from, or what they believe.

Ultimately, I hope you'll be inspired to make a difference in the world by investing in the relationships you already have and building new ones. Why emphasize relationships? Because relationships are where you and I live. Our relationships are the context of our lives. No matter how introverted or extroverted we might be, we're still relational beings. God created us to relate to one another all the days of our lives. We should boldly and graciously engage and invest our faith in our relationships, regardless of whether we disagree with someone else on politics, ethics, or who should have won the award for best picture.

I can guarantee you this: if the way we invest in the people around us improves, it won't be long before we start changing the world, one relationship at a time. However, that will never happen if we allow fear to compromise the difference we could make.

It's time we turn our attention to something more powerful than our fears of tomorrow. We need a perspective that's greater than any anxiety we may face. The good news for us is that there is something more powerful than the worst fears that linger in our heads. Actually, let me say that differently: there is *someone* greater than our worst fears, and that someone deserves the priority in our perspectives.

REFLECTION AND DISCUSSION QUESTIONS

1. What changes do you see in society that cause you fear? Why do they cause you fear?

2. How do you interact with society? Option A, B, or C? Do you think you're interacting with society in the right way? Why or why not?

3. Have you seen any of your family, friends, or acquaintances do extraordinary things? What did they do?

4. The God of Tomorrow principle is, *Since tomorrow belongs to God, we can graciously offer hope to people today.* Do you believe this is true? Is this statement reflected in how you live your life?

5. Spend some time in prayer before moving on to the next chapter. Ask God to open your heart to what he might want you to learn, affirm, or stop or start doing as you consider the intersection of your faith and society.

SURRENDER TOMORROW TO GOD— HE'S ALREADY BEEN THERE.

2

God Isn't Afraid

Why are *you* afraid of tomorrow, especially as it relates to changes in our cultural climate? What worries you and keeps you up at night?

If you're fearful and anxious—for whatever reason—I don't want to pile guilt on you about that. You're hardly alone! Whether you're from Japan or the Dominican Republic, a man or woman, Democrat or Republican, Southern Baptist or United Methodist, there are plenty of catalysts in life that can provoke emotions of fear. More than you know, I have my periods of discouragement and worry too. *Today* seems to provide so many valid reasons for us to worry about *tomorrow*.

As you woke up this morning, maybe you were excited to begin the day. Unfortunately, the decision to check your favorite news app caused you to exchange your excitement for anxiety. Once again our nation is facing significant upheaval, and now that's all you can think about. Your day has barely started and has officially been ruined.

Perhaps your reality is that you've been searching diligently for work ever since you lost your job, but no employer is giving you a second look. Meanwhile, you hear people talk about "the illegals" who come to our country and "steal our jobs." Now your frustration has a focal point. As a result, however unintentionally, you've mentally and unfairly stockpiled people into a single category.

Or upon getting home from work, you find your daughter crying on the sofa. Your conversation with her reveals the problem: for the first time, someone was racist toward her. Even though you try to comfort her, bitterness and distress become your companions again as you're brought back to similar experiences in your life.

Plenty of evangelical and conservative Christians have a strong fear of tomorrow because of society's growing intolerance of their theological convictions. Some apparently would be happier if they could put a muzzle on the prophetic voice of the church.

Whatever the nature of your fear about tomorrow, my goal is to help you see the value in shifting your focus. The only way to counter our fear of tomorrow is to stop focusing on what tomorrow *might* deliver. Otherwise, our fear manifests itself in the destructive emotion of worry. The effect that worry has on us and around us is far more damaging than most comprehend.

Newt Scamander is one of the heroes in the movie *Fantastic Beasts and Where to Find Them*. I won't give away the plot, but he makes a difference wherever he goes and does so with humility and wisdom. Throughout the movie, he shares his wisdom with some of the other characters. One of the pearls of wisdom Newt drops in the movie is spot on: "My philosophy is that worrying means you suffer twice."[1]

Our fear is no match for the unlimited power and uncontested reign of God.

He's right. Worry is harmful. But thankfully, as natural as worry is, we don't need to dwell there. As another man who went about doing good and offering wisdom once said, "Do not worry about tomorrow, for tomorrow will worry about itself" (Matthew 6:34). I think we can trust him on that (and anything else). God isn't afraid of tomorrow, and neither should we be.

The principle underlying this book is, *Since tomorrow belongs to God, we can graciously offer hope to people today.* But we can do that only when hope dwells within us.

Though Christians have differing views on God's sovereignty, most of us who follow Jesus would readily agree that tomorrow (the future) belongs to God. While we might theologically believe that God is in control, that same belief may not have taken up residence in our hearts. Why? Too often, our fears take precedence over our trust in God. Such a problem begs the question, how do we begin to move past our fears? What will it take for us to look beyond the instability of today and pessimism of tomorrow? More than likely, it comes down to a choice we must make. You and I need to make the decision to either surrender to our fear or continually trust God. My opinion: our fear is no match for the unlimited power and uncontested reign of God.

When you think of power, what comes to mind? Specifically, who or what are you assuming is going to be responsible for how tomorrow turns out? Is it politicians? Corporations? Advertisers? Some political party or political action committee? A foreign dictator? Or _____? (You fill in the blank.)

Our view of what power is and who has it is a determining factor for how we live and think about society. It will dictate how we respond in difficult situations. The Gospels give us an example of this from the day when Jesus was crucified. Jesus stood on trial before Pontius Pilate, who was the Roman governor at that time, and the two of them had quite an interesting exchange of words. We need to take a look at part of their conversation.

WHERE POWER COMES FROM

The Jewish leaders had brought Jesus to the Roman governor, charging Jesus with wanting to become king of the Jewish people in place of the Roman emperor. Pilate, however, wasn't really concerned about the supposed threat Jesus represented to Roman power. So, near the end of the dialogue between Jesus and Pilate, we see Pilate trying to free Jesus as best he politically can because he knew that Jesus had committed no crime.

But why didn't he just release Jesus and move on with the day? Pilate was surrounded with an angry crowd demanding the death of Jesus, and he didn't want any problems or an uproar. In other words, Pilate feared a violent riot more than he regretted the death of an innocent person.

Pilate was a coward, but a shrewd one. As some politicians do, he tried to find the middle ground. But there would be no middle ground here. Controlled by the religious leaders of their day (a.k.a. the Pharisees and enemies of Jesus), this crowd chanted, "Crucify, crucify!" It would take only a little prompting from the Pharisees, and the crowd would start to be aggressive. While the Roman soldiers could undoubtedly get the upper hand on the situation, they wouldn't be able to do so without killing many people.

Even the deaths of a few people in Roman territory weren't good for the imperial rule. The slightest rebellion could ignite a fire that might grow into something the soldiers couldn't extinguish. Pilate knew if there was too much discord from the people he oversaw, the Roman emperor could reassign him to a less desirable location, remove his authority, or even execute him. Pilate was allowing his fear of what tomorrow *might* bring to jeopardize the decision he knew was right: to free an innocent man.

Attempting to spare Jesus from crucifixion while safeguarding himself, Pilate asked the crowd to accept the death of a criminal instead of

Jesus. In hopes of further appeasing the crowd, Pilate also had Jesus flogged and gave a shot at reasoning with the incensed group of individuals. Then, frustrated with all this, he asked a very important question of Jesus and received an answer that was deeper than he expected. "Where do you come from?" Pilate asked Jesus (John 19:9).

What did Jesus say to this?

Nothing.

I guess he wasn't eager to pretend that this circus would ensure a fair trial.

Pilate wouldn't let it go. In verse 10, he continued and said, "Do you refuse to speak to me? . . . Don't you realize I have power either to free you or to crucify you?"

Jesus had an answer to this, and as we see in verse 11, it was a bold one: "You would have no power over me if it were not given to you from above."

God has all the power and calls the shots.

Forget tomorrow for a moment. How was Jesus able to lay down any crippling fear of what was going to happen on *that very day*? He believed all power was given "from above"—that is, from God the Father. Jesus was telling Pilate that his power as a Roman governor was limited because the authority "from above" was calling the shots in that moment.

In saying this, Jesus wasn't proclaiming anything different from what the rest of Scripture tells us: God has all the power and calls the shots.

God is so immense that it's difficult to describe him, but the writers of the Bible give us a glimpse. In one instance, Paul began to describe God at the beginning of his first letter to Timothy: "To the King eternal, immortal, invisible, the only God, be honor and glory for ever and ever" (1:17). From this we learn the following about God:

- He is "the King" and "the only God." He is divinely sovereign—the only one who is.
- He is "eternal, immortal." He is without a beginning or end. There has never been a time when God was not. God hasn't ever had a birthday party or a retirement party. He just *is*.
- He is "invisible." He isn't composed of matter and isn't limited by physical dimensions as we are.

That is a brief New Testament example of how the Bible tries to describe God's almighty power. Here's one from the Old Testament:

> Remember the former things, those of long ago;
>   I am God, and there is no other;
>   I am God, and there is none like me.
> I make known the end from the beginning,
>   from ancient times, what is still to come.
> I say, "My purpose will stand,
>   and I will do all that I please." (Isaiah 46:9–10)

In other words, because God alone is divine and eternal, his will encompasses everything that has ever happened, is happening, or will happen. He could tell us in detail "the end from the beginning," the past from the future, yesterday from tomorrow. Nothing surprises him. Nothing is outside the scope of his might and control.

Life seems chaotic? The world appears to be spinning out of control? Tomorrow looms with threats? Society shows every sign of morphing into something that feels alien to you? A leader who stands for everything you disagree with has just been elected to office? Well, God is still unhindered and has complete jurisdiction over all things. He is molding the events in society to serve a purpose that's greater than any one person, greater than any one society, greater than any one generation. Sooner or later, everyone will discover what Jesus spoke about to Pilate: *true power comes from above.*

A KING DISCOVERS THE KING

Back in Old Testament times, a prophet of God named Daniel lived in exile within a city called Babylon. This society had values that make the United States seem like Disney World. At that time, the king of the Babylonian Empire was named Nebuchadnezzar. If there was ever a narcissist, it was this guy. His egotism reached a point where God had enough and dealt with it—so you know his pride was definitely bad.

Daniel 4 teaches that one day Nebuchadnezzar was walking on the roof of his palace, surveying his kingdom, and thinking about how he deserved all the fame for how large his empire had become. (Spoiler alert: God thought otherwise.)

Earlier in the story, Daniel had to tell the king that he would be forced out of his position in Babylon for a few years so he could be reminded of who was in control and who was not. To drive the point home, these are some of the things the prophet said to Nebuchadnezzar:

> The Most High is sovereign over all kingdoms on earth and
> gives them to anyone he wishes and sets over them the lowliest
> of people. . . .
>
> Seven times will pass by for you until you acknowledge that
> the Most High is sovereign over all kingdoms on earth and gives
> them to anyone he wishes. . . . Your kingdom will be restored to
> you when you acknowledge that Heaven rules. (verses 17, 25–26)

On behalf of God, Daniel basically told Nebuchadnezzar that earthly leaders really don't have the power they think they have but that God does have all power. God alone decides who has earthly authority, who doesn't, who keeps it, who loses it, and who finds it. Of course, the king didn't get what Daniel was saying, so he was driven out of his kingdom and treated like an animal.

After years of being humbled by living as an animal, Nebuchadnezzar had a change of heart. He eventually testified:

> I, Nebuchadnezzar, raised my eyes toward heaven, and my sanity was restored. Then I praised the Most High; I honored and glorified him who lives forever.
>
> His dominion is an eternal dominion;
>> his kingdom endures from generation to generation.
> All the peoples of the earth
>> are regarded as nothing.
> He does as he pleases
>> with the powers of heaven
>> and the peoples of the earth.
> No one can hold back his hand
>> or say to him: "What have you done?" (verses 34–35)

Notice what the king admits:
- God lives forever; he doesn't.
- God's dominion is eternal; he isn't.
- God's kingdom endures; he won't.
- God has true authority; he doesn't.
- God does as he pleases; he can't.
- God cannot be chided; he can.

For me, King Nebuchadnezzar's last statement of Daniel 4 is what's so powerful. "I, Nebuchadnezzar, praise and exalt and glorify the King of heaven, because everything he does is right and all his ways are just" (verse 37). Or as one of the professors at my seminary used to say, "God has the 'right to rule.'"[2]

I'm *not* saying it's always easy to remember that God is in control and rules over all. Again, Christians might theologically understand that he is all powerful and all loving. But in human hearts, where fear dwells, we aren't always so sure. Our faith in God's sovereignty and love is challenged whenever things in life go horribly wrong. That's true for our personal problems as well as for the heartbreaking tragedies that take place in society.

UNDENIABLY DEPENDABLE

Whenever I think of one week in July 2016, I am reminded of how sad, how unnecessarily sad, our society can be. These are the times when we ask, "God, where are you in this?"

On July 5 an African American man named Alton Sterling was shot and killed by a police officer outside a convenience store in Baton Rouge, Louisiana. A video of the shooting surfaced and added even more emotion to the tragedy. Some came to the officer's defense, while others claimed racism to be the reason for the shooting.

Unfortunately, the next day proved to be just as bad.

Another African American gentleman, Philando Castile, was shot and killed by a police officer in St. Anthony, Minnesota. Castile was pulled over as part of a traffic stop, and a video was released that showed him after the shooting. He was moaning in the last moments of his life, and his girlfriend was terrified, as was her four-year-old daughter in the back seat. Voices, anger, and sadness rose even more among the American people in conversations and social media.

The following day brought even more tragedy.

In Dallas, Texas, on July 7, a protest was held because of the shootings. During the protest, Micah Xavier Johnson opened fire on the crowd with a rifle. When the shots rang out, chaos filled the streets. Two witnesses described the commotion. One said, "I was screaming, 'Run! Run! Active shooter! Run!' And I was trying to get folks out as fast as I could." Another said, "Everyone was screaming, people were running. I saw at least probably 30 shots go off."[3]

By the end of the night, five police officers were killed, nine people were wounded, and the gunman was killed. America was even more broken.

Needless to say, that was one of the more difficult weeks our society has seen. Fear surged in our land. Once again, tomorrow proved to be unpredictable. Once again, society changed that week.

But here's where I need to point out a contrast. I want to offer you some encouragement and build up your faith in God the King *regardless of what happens in life.* As I mentioned in the first chapter, society will change again and again, but God remains ever the same.

How many of us have broken promises we've made? How many of us have experienced broken trust from someone we love? Pretty sure we all have. But in Numbers 23:19, Moses said, "God is not human, that he should lie, not a human being, that he should change his mind." People change, but not God.

Unlike the gods of Greek mythology, God is never capricious. The prophet Samuel said God "does not lie or change his mind; for he is not a human being, that he should change his mind" (1 Samuel 15:29). He "does not change like shifting shadows" (James 1:17). God doesn't go in one direction and then shift gears out of impulse. He is completely dependable.

As plainly as possible, God declares, "I the LORD do not change" (Malachi 3:6). And the implications of a God who doesn't change are enormous. If God always remains the same, then regardless of what occurs in society, he keeps promises to journey with us in life. He has the same concerns he's always had, while maintaining the same level of ethics and morals he's always had. Nothing thwarts his plans for the good. Therefore, the dominating attitude of our lives can be something other than worry.

REAL HOPE

With a God who has our back, we've got little to worry about. Paul assured us of the uselessness of worry when he wrote Philippians 4:6–7: "Do not be anxious about anything, but in every situation, by prayer and petition, with thanksgiving, present your requests to God. And the peace of God, which transcends all understanding, will guard your hearts and your minds in Christ Jesus."

God has tomorrow under control because he's the wisest and most capable being in existence. He is fully loving, gracious, and merciful, and he is personally involved in the lives of his followers. His unequaled power has important ramifications not only for our lives but also for our interaction with society.

We can boldly and graciously offer hope to people today because God has created and prepared tomorrow, and he will walk with us into it. Since God is supreme and has all power, we should refuse to grant fear the luxury of controlling our next steps. I'm convinced that the biggest implication God's sovereignty has for our lives today is *hope*.

We desperately need hope. When we talk about the word *hope,* we usually equate it to wishful thinking. We'll say things such as, "We *hope* they accept our bid on the house we want" or "I *hope* I get the job I interviewed for." In our culture, hope has become synonymous with wishing or aspiring. But that wasn't always the case.

Our expectant hope is that God has the path laid out before us, will journey with us, and already knows what tomorrow holds.

The word *hope* has more depth in the Bible. The authors of the Bible understood the word *hope* to be the expectancy of a promised outcome or the waiting period before a promise was carried out. Writers such as Paul also believed that hope originated from God and was assured by his supremacy and the strength of his integrity. That's why Paul said in Romans 5:5 that hope *doesn't shame us.* The hope that society longs for is found in God, who walks with us in life. The hope he offers will counter our fear and worry about the future. Our expectant hope is that God has the path laid out before us, will journey with us, and already knows what tomorrow holds.

Where do you need hope right now? What are you worried about? Are there disturbing trends in society that look irreversible to you? Do you think society won't recover lost values that are important to you? Have you felt powerless and hopeless in the face of some specific societal changes? *Even there* you can have hope, not because a future elected official or a boycott or a social crusade might reverse the situation, but because God is working out what is best in his time. He has promised the restoration of all things according to what is right, and he will do it.

As I mentioned, I became a follower of Jesus as a teenager. After that,

I attended a nearby Bible college with ministry in mind. But I never really understood the biblical concept of hope until after I finished college and was on my own for the first time.

HOPE TESTED TO THE LIMIT

When I was young and single, I moved to Southern California to work at Shepherd Church, even though I didn't know many people in that area. Eventually I became friends with a couple of guys from the church and the three of us rented a house together. Having a bachelor pad was fun— late nights, tons of jokes, and inappropriate pranks galore. After a couple of years, one of my roommates got married and moved about fifteen minutes away from our bachelor pad. I wasn't surprised that he got married so quickly—he was the opposite of me in almost every way you could think: tall, good looking, lots of hair, in shape, tan, and he even worked for the Drug Enforcement Administration as an agent. When we were roommates, I was convinced I'd be beaten up by drug lords, much like Joe Pesci was in *Lethal Weapon 3*. After that roommate got married, eventually the other one and I went our separate ways.

About a year later, one evening near the end of October, I got one of those late-night phone calls that no one wants to receive. My roommate who had gotten married had been killed in a motorcycle accident. He had been riding his motorcycle down a residential street that evening when another driver made an illegal U-turn. My roommate's motorcycle T-boned the car, throwing him from his bike and hurling him into eternity. It was horrific.

I arrived at the accident scene about thirty minutes after the call. Much of the site had been cleaned up already, but my friend's bike was still in the middle of the street. It was absolutely destroyed. Friends who had gotten the same call that I had started arriving. After a while, many of us went down the street to his house. His young widow was at home, understandably crying her eyes out. The setting of the house gave the false impression that he'd be right back. His drink was still on the counter, clothes were laid on the bed for tomorrow, the TV was on, and his book was in his chair. I half expected him to walk in the door, but I knew that wasn't going to happen.

I sat in his house with fifteen other people for about three hours. No one really said anything. There were lots of hugs and sobbing, but no conversations. Every person in that room was a follower of Jesus, so we prayed. We weren't even sure what to pray, but we prayed.

A couple of weeks later, we had the memorial service and graveside observance. I still remember the graveside as if it were yesterday. I've attended many gravesides, but I've never seen as many people stay for the entire covering of the casket as did for my roommate's. It was as if none of us wanted to leave, because if we left, we were submitting to the reality that he was gone from this earth.

Before I left the graveside, my eyes looked beyond the freeways of Hollywood and fixated on the hills behind Burbank. Clouds began forming behind the hills and started moving almost on top of them. I don't know how clearly you can picture it, but it was a dramatic scene that touched my already emotional heart. In that moment, I fervently asked Jesus to come back. But I knew there was a good chance that my timing wasn't his.

I did, however, gain a perspective of hope that day. As I gazed at the hills, I was reminded that the power of God will be seen in supreme majesty when Jesus returns to bring justice, order, and redemption to this world. Closing my eyes, I remembered Paul's description of Jesus's return:

> The trumpet will sound, the dead will be raised imperishable, and
> we will be changed. For the perishable must clothe itself with the

imperishable, and the mortal with immortality. When the
perishable has been clothed with the imperishable, and the
mortal with immortality, then the saying that is written
will come true: "Death has been swallowed up in victory."
(1 Corinthians 15:52–54)

Imagining what it would be like on the last day when my roommate
would be brought into his new God-given body provided hope. I still have
that hope because I believe that my God is powerful enough to bring Jesus
back from the dead and will do the same for those who follow him. As
much as I loathe death, I know that it won't have the last laugh. God's
greatness deserves our trust and willingness to align our lives to his power.
The hope he gives extends beyond the circumstances of society and the
inconsistency of our lives. Only he has the power to give us such hope.

Better Begins with Us

The Bible gives us a powerful promise that one day a greater tomorrow
will arrive and we will all live in it. The power of God points us to a hope
that is found in what he will do in the greatest tomorrow we can imagine!
So whatever our tomorrow delivers, whether it's good news or tragedy, we
will make it through because God holds tomorrow and will walk with us
into tomorrow. He created and prepared tomorrow.

Let me ask you: Do you believe this? Are you truly convinced that
God is all powerful, has a plan for redemption, and is guiding us into a
better tomorrow? Do you have faith that when horrible things happen in
our world, God works them out for the good? I'm sure you would say yes
(even though we've all had our moments of doubt). By the way, I would
answer yes as well. But if I believe that God is sovereign and owns tomorrow, why doesn't my life always reflect it? While I understand there are

some who have clinical depression and other diagnosed disorders, overall I believe that my worry can be a barometer of my faith and trust in God. I always wonder how my life would be different if I truly lived as if God already has my path planned. I'm sure there's a good chance you've wondered the same thing about yourself. In those moments when worry starts to rise and faith begins to fall, I must remind myself to go back and read about the power of God. Whether those are verses that describe God or stories in the Bible that build my trust in his power despite overwhelming odds, I'm comforted when I get done reading about his faithfulness.

Along with reading about God's power, I have to be consistent in my daily prayer time. If I'm not spending time talking with God and listening for him, how in the world will I trust him? Similarly, I set aside some time to think about and remember all the times in the past when God has been faithful to me. He's seen me through some pretty dark hours. When I can decrease the worry and increase my faith, it allows me to remember that God is in control and already has a plan toward tomorrow. But the problem with worry is that it doesn't only decrease my faith; it compromises the influence I can have in the lives of others. Having high faith and low worry takes my eyes off myself so I can do what God wants me to do: *graciously offer hope to people today.*

Hope reminds us that our best days are ahead, not behind us.

With boldness and graciousness as our allies, let's confidently point people in the direction of what hope has to offer: God himself. He himself is the focal point that we look to when we're fatigued, upset, saddened, or troubled about the coming days. Hope reminds us that our best days are ahead, not behind us.

This is so crucial for us because, as we'll talk about later, things won't "get better." We aren't going to rewind to thirty years ago. The people, cities, and towns surrounding us are continually progressing. No politician will be able to take the White House or governor's mansion and then create the kind of government that would make everyone feel comfortable. Bullying will continue to find new ways to raise its ugly head. Regrettably, we still have people in our society who are homeless and have little or no access to help. War and terror are ripping our world apart. Sickness, disease, discrimination, and starvation seem to have no end. Instead of entertaining delusions of grandeur, maybe the hope of a greater tomorrow can fuel our engagement of society with the gospel. Things in our society won't ever be perfect (though one day God will bring a perfect world into existence), but God can certainly make things better today. And better begins with us.

There's no reason to be afraid if you serve the God who has all power and has vowed to be with you throughout your life. Whatever fears you might have of other people, trusting God and his power can begin to kill such fears. Are you afraid of tough conversations with people who have a different ethic than you? When you ask God for strength in your discussions with others, he will be there with you. Do you have misguided and wrong stereotypes of people in different economic classes than you? Don't be afraid, and ask God to eliminate that sinful fear from your heart. If he is sovereign and created all people, then he created the people you fear just as he created you. While you must be careful with people who hurt you, why would you unnaturally fear another human being that God created?

Hope means that whatever tomorrow holds, our fear isn't required.

True hope assures us that God holds tomorrow.

Surrender tomorrow to God—he's already been there.

REFLECTION AND DISCUSSION QUESTIONS

1. Read the interaction between Jesus and Pilate again. Notice that Pilate allowed his fear to direct his decisions. What happened because of Pilate surrendering to his fear? Has there been a time when you allowed your fear to control you? What happened?

2. What does God say about himself and his power in Isaiah 46:9–10?

3. People and society are constantly changing. However, according to Numbers 23:19, 1 Samuel 15:29, Malachi 3:6, and James 1:17, God never changes. He is completely consistent. What are the implications of an unchanging God as we live in an ever-changing world?

4. Read Philippians 4:6–7. What does Paul say about being anxious and how to reduce anxiety? Now read 1 Corinthians 15:52–54 and reflect on our hope for when the world around us seems chaotic.

5. If you had no fear, what would you do for God?

LIFE GAINS CLARITY WHEN WE DISCOVER—OR REDISCOVER—THAT OUR IDENTITY IS ROOTED IN GOD.

3

Leverage the Relationship

In the previous chapter, we saw that God is all powerful, is completely caring, and never changes. If we as Christians want to engage society effectively, we have to attach ourselves firmly to God and leverage our relationship with Jesus to help others. The more I process this idea, the more convinced I am that we cannot leverage our relationship with Jesus without trusting God to be sovereign. This will give us a solid selfhood that doesn't shift with the tides of change. There might be people on the left who criticize our commitment to "outdated" biblical morality or people on the right who question our rigorous care and concern for people. But if we know who we are in God through Christ, we can survive the tension. In fact, we won't be much use to society unless our faith, empowered by our relationship with Jesus, brings a contrast to society's changeable and variable nature.

It's also important to anchor ourselves as close to God as we can because as we approach tomorrow in a shifting society, we can easily drift away from him. Even though we follow Jesus and have been redeemed by grace, we're constantly tempted to be drawn back into our old way of life. It's all too easy to gravitate toward what sounds right or feels good in the moment. Surrendering to our momentary desires prompts us to forget the importance of our relationship with Jesus. To say it another way, our faith can easily become more self-determined instead of being God derived. Practically, if not openly, we start focusing on ourselves again instead of God. This is something we have to fight against if we're going to strengthen our relationship with Jesus.

You see, whether you realize it or not, your relationship with Jesus isn't just a benefit to you. When it comes to how you leverage and grow in your relationship with Jesus, more hangs in the balance than what you might be aware of. God takes his relationship with us seriously, not just because he loves us but also because our relationship with Jesus can be used for more than just our eternal life—a lot more. To see what I'm talking about here, we need to turn our attention to a person in the Bible who was blinded by the light.

THE TOXIN INSIDE

When we first meet Paul in the New Testament, he actually has a different name: Saul. He also has a very different attitude toward people than he did when he wrote his New Testament letters. We're joining Saul at a time in his life when he's an aspiring religious leader who's filled with ambition and willing to do whatever he can to make people follow God or pay!

In Acts 7:58, the first Christian martyr, Stephen, was condemned to death for his faith. People laid their cloaks at the feet of Saul, picked up rocks, and killed Stephen. The fact that people were laying down their coats at the feet of Saul is symbolic that he was taking responsibility for Stephen's death.

Acts 9:1–2 gives us our second look at Saul:

Meanwhile, Saul was still breathing out murderous threats against the Lord's disciples. He went to the high priest and asked him for letters to the synagogues in Damascus, so that if he found any

there who belonged to the Way, whether men or women,
he might take them as prisoners to Jerusalem.

Let's make some observations about Saul. First, he was filled with pride that led to selfishness. He wanted and then achieved influence with religious leaders and others in authority, and he obtained their permission to persecute Christians and bring them to trial—all in the name of God. He thought he was serving God, but he had no idea who God had revealed himself to be, and he worked for his own gain.

Before we're too tough on Saul, we should probably admit we're not that different. While I agree we may not have attempted to kill or imprison Christians, we can still relate to him. Our first inclination is to look out for number one (a.k.a. self). I guarantee that every parent understands that his or her child never had to learn to be selfish. To see this illustrated even more blatantly, wait in a line for a sporting event, major movie premiere, amusement park ride, checkout at a grocery store, or really any line of your choice. You'll see that sinful nature at work! Go to an Oakland Raiders game in a Kansas City Chiefs jersey. Listen to some of the conversations in the church parking lot after church. Pay attention to the attitudes of people in the grocery store on Saturday morning . . . You get the point.

Saul was not only selfish; he was also *combative*. He was fighting against society so he could make a difference for God. Saul didn't care who he arrested or hurt in the process, which families were torn apart, or even if Jesus followers were correct in their thinking—he wanted to lock them away. It made no difference to him that the society of his day was broken and hurting (just like ours is). Saul leveraged his religious standing to make a stand for God, no matter who got hurt in the process. Basically, he was looking out for himself while trying to impress God and others at the same time.

This is one of those moments when you and I need to pause for a moment of self-reflection. If we're Jesus followers, how do we approach society? Do we do so with courage and graciousness so we can offer hope, or do we approach society with the goal of just being theologically *correct*? Are we willing to use our social media feed, email forwards, and passive-aggressive comments in conversations with people who have different outlooks on life so we can just be heard?

To be combative toward a broken society, you have to be selfish. It's impossible to be hurtful toward a broken society that Jesus gave his life for and not be "in it to win it" for yourself. The problem is that like us, Saul, in his religiosity and self-righteousness, had no idea how toxic he really was.

Everyone you know (including you) is full of poison. There are really two kinds of dangerous people: those who know how toxic they are and those who don't.

Have you ever heard of the poison dart frog? If not, let me describe it. This creature is small, cute, and colorful like a bag of Skittles—and some varieties are among the deadliest creatures on the earth. All you have to do is touch some of these frogs and you're done. It's over. You're in harp land. If their poison gets in you, people will be at your funeral a few days later and eating potato salad with your friends afterward. I'm sure the frog has no idea how toxic it is, and the truth is that most people have no idea how toxic they are.

But God didn't create us to be toxic. When humanity fell and sin entered the world, our very nature became toxic and we forgot who God really was. The sin of humanity altered the identity that God gave us. We aren't who we think we are.

Martin Heidegger was a German philosopher in the twentieth century, and some of his research was on how society progresses with technology and other advancements. He believed that society actually gets worse, not better, as it progresses. In his opinion, people's essential identity "can be covered up to such a degree that it is forgotten and the question about it and its meaning altogether omitted."[1]

The biggest obstacle between society and Jesus followers is us—you and me.

I'm my own biggest obstacle to the influence I want to build with others. Nearly the entire remainder of the book will be focused on that obstacle. Why? No one else can compromise my bold voice and gracious posture as I can. My sinful insecurities, such as selfishness and combativeness, are just waiting for the times when my trust in God weakens. In those vulnerable moments, I'm prone to being ungracious and slanderous, giving in to toxic anxiety, lashing out in anger, holding on to offenses, seeking my own interests, and . . . well, you get the picture.

> ## The biggest obstacle between society and Jesus followers is us—you and me.

Isn't it strange that you and I as believers in Jesus would act like this? I mean, we've been redeemed, right? We've supposedly been changed on the inside—and we have been and still are changing. But the toxins of sin linger in our system and are strong enough to do a lot of harm. Saul was about to learn this lesson the hard way.

When the Light Comes On

As Saul got closer to Damascus, he was probably thinking about how many Jesus followers he could arrest, what kind of accolades he'd receive if he captured many of those people, and so on. His mind was probably lost in the clouds of his own thinking when something amazing happened to him.

> As he neared Damascus on his journey, suddenly a light from heaven flashed around him. He fell to the ground and heard a voice say to him, "Saul, Saul, why do you persecute me?"
>
> "Who are you, Lord?" Saul asked.
>
> "I am Jesus, whom you are persecuting," he replied. "Now get up and go into the city, and you will be told what you must do."
>
> The men traveling with Saul stood there speechless; they heard the sound but did not see anyone. (Acts 9:3–7)

Verses 8–9 say that "Saul got up from the ground, but when he opened his eyes he could see nothing. So they led him by the hand into Damascus. For three days he was blind, and did not eat or drink anything."

God has done some amazing things in three days: darkness covered Egypt for three days (Exodus 10:22–23), Jonah was in the belly of a fish for three days and preached in Nineveh for three days (Jonah 1:17; 3:3), Jesus rose from the dead after three days (Matthew 26:61; 27:40), and so on. Many of these instances in the Bible were days of waiting, reflection, silence, repenting—all while God was moving. The three days Saul had to himself after he saw Jesus were no different.

Can you imagine what Saul was thinking over those three days? He was brilliant and knew the Old Testament scriptures like the back of his hand. I suppose his mind was going over Old Testament promises about the Messiah and considering how they related to Jesus. I'm sure Saul kept thinking about how wrong he was about God. Then, I bet, he began to remember the innocent people he had captured or jailed or whose deaths he had even presided at. Up to this point in Saul's life, he more than likely believed that his persecution of Christians was actually serving God and helping society. But now things were different. Saul had seen Jesus, discovered who Jesus was, learned more about God than he had bargained for, and understood that he was on the wrong side of God. I really believe that for one of the first times, Saul realized how toxic he was. He understood that he was the problem, not others.

As a fan of the Rocky movies, I thought the movie *Creed* was a great addition to the Rocky Balboa universe. If you're not familiar with the movie, Rocky ends up training a guy named Adonis for a boxing match. Adonis is the son of the deceased Apollo Creed, Rocky's friend and trainer and a former heavyweight champ.

During one scene, Rocky and Adonis are standing in front of a mirror in the gym during their training session. Rocky teaches Adonis a brilliant lesson about self-perception. Pointing at Adonis in the mirror, Rocky says, "You see this guy here staring back at you?"

"Yeah," Adonis answers.

"That's your toughest opponent. Every time you get into the ring, that's who you're going against. I believe that in boxing, and I do believe that in life."[2]

Rocky Balboa—the "Italian Stallion" boxing philosopher! I don't know about you, but I agree with Rocky. While we definitely face tough times in society (we'll be continuing to talk about some of these tough times), there's no adversary comparable to the one we see looking back at us in the mirror.

When Adonis learns this important principle, the movie shifts and he begins to see boxing and life differently. We need to take a cue from Adonis in this moment. I'm not implying we should despise ourselves. Not at all. Rather, I believe that I am my biggest enemy and you are your biggest enemy. Society is full of people, and each person is his or her own worst enemy. God allows the mirror to be held up to us sometimes so we can remember who we are and who he is.

I've been there before. Have you? I remember one particular moment in my life when someone held the mirror up to me for the first time. Several years ago I was sitting at a table in a coffee shop with my friend, and my head was in my hands. It was late morning and the sun was shining through the windows. People all around us were having conversations, ordering drinks, laughing at jokes, catching up, and so on. All these people seemed to be going about their lives oblivious to me, a person who was struggling.

"Caleb, look at me. *Caleb?*" my friend said.

I could barely hear his voice because of the questions swirling in my head. *How did I get to this point? What happened?*

A couple of days earlier, I began dealing with a situation at the church I was leading at the time. The situation had me hurting and wondering what God wanted us to do as a church. Hurt feelings, misunderstandings, and the like comprised the scenario. I wasn't sure what tomorrow would hold for the church and me.

"Look at me," my friend said again.

I lifted my head out of the palms of my hands and stared at him. He looked at me with a reassuring smile and said some words I will never forget. "Caleb, remember who you are."

It was almost as if a light went on in my head. I paused, leaned back, and stared at him. As I was staring at him, I felt as though he had gotten a mirror and held it up in front of me.

I had forgotten who I was. In a weird way, I was keeping myself from trusting God.

At some point in my spiritual journey, as I made my way to the situation I was facing in that instance, I had created a false identity and began drawing my worth from my work, not from God. I didn't place important boundaries in my life. I couldn't see that my insecurity had reduced God to the role of distant uncle rather than loving Father. I acted as if family was number one, but I had forgotten to place them there. For a while, they just got emotional leftovers. I assumed I had countless friends, but I didn't realize how shallow I'd become in my interactions with people.

Life gains clarity when we discover—or rediscover—that our identity is rooted in God.

God had had enough of my performance. You see, he cares too much about his followers not to hold the mirror up to our faces. He felt it was time for me to remember who I was. I had been living behind a mask for far too long. I was still a believer in Jesus, but I was a believer who had misplaced his identity and was in need of a reminder. Life gains clarity when we discover—or rediscover—that our identity is rooted in God. When I was in that coffee shop, God needed to break my pride. For Saul, it took three days for his pride to be broken, and then it was time for Jesus to step in.

AND THEN JESUS STEPPED IN

According to Acts 9:10–15, Jesus miraculously called on one of his followers, Ananias, to go baptize Saul. At first Ananias didn't want to because he knew that Saul arrested people like him. Can you blame him? But Jesus assured Ananias that he had called Saul to follow him and urged him to go ahead and baptize Saul.

Ananias obeyed Jesus and eventually found the place where Saul was staying.

Ananias went to the house and entered it. Placing his hands on Saul, he said, "Brother Saul, the Lord—Jesus, who appeared to you on the road as you were coming here—has sent me so that you may see again and be filled with the Holy Spirit." Immediately, something like scales fell from Saul's eyes, and he could see again. He got up and was baptized, and after taking some food, he regained his strength. (verses 17–19)

Whenever I read or listen to this story, I'm still blown away by how instantaneous Saul's recovery was. He saw Jesus, went blind, waited for three days, reached a point where he believed in Jesus as the Messiah, was baptized, and regained his strength. Truly, Jesus completes God's revelation of himself to us. Before Saul became a Christian, he had an incomplete understanding of who God really was. Once Saul started following Jesus, his idea of God became complete. His vision of Jesus in the beginning of Acts 9 allowed him to be able to see God as he truly is. And when Jesus intersects with your life and completes your image of God, your life begins to change.

How did Saul change? According to Acts 9:20–29, Saul immediately started preaching about Jesus (verse 20), grew more powerful (verse 22), started proving that Jesus was the Messiah (verse 22), gained followers (verse 25), received Christian allies (verse 27), wasn't ashamed of being a Christian (verse 28), and debated with others about faith (verse 29). In other words, Saul

- became bold about his faith instead of keeping the law
- found his power through his faith, not in his authority
- showed people how Jesus gives hope
- had people follow him instead of run from him
- took pride in his faith

Martin Heidegger (the German philosopher I mentioned earlier) was asked in an interview what solution would fix society's identity problem. His reply is more than a little interesting: "Only a god can save us."[3] He was right and wrong at the same time. We need divine intervention, but there's no such thing as *a god;* we need *the only true God* to step in and save us. He's all powerful, and his supremacy knows no end. And he sent Jesus to give us not only a hope for tomorrow but also strength for this present time.

Besides the fact that a relationship with Jesus saved Saul, it helped him to have an impact for Jesus in the lives of those around him: "Then the church throughout Judea, Galilee and Samaria enjoyed a time of peace and was strengthened. Living in the fear of the Lord and encouraged by the Holy Spirit, it increased in numbers" (verse 31).

Saul's relationship with Jesus had an impact on more than just his own personal hope and salvation; it influenced those he was in contact with. He leveraged his new relationship with Jesus to help those in his society see the hope God had to offer. When Saul was giving into selfishness and being combative with society, he was operating from fear—which brought conflict and pain. Later when Saul became a Christian and his engagement of people was fueled by his trust in God, he was filled with courage and brought hope to people. God changed Saul's name to Paul, and he became a church planter, preacher, missionary, biblical author, elder, and trusted friend of many. He was willing to look in the mirror, consider God, and then follow Jesus for the rest of his life.

Jesus not only completes our idea of who God is and saves us but also is with us today. Jesus is God's all-powerful answer to society's chaos. Following him gives us the opportunity to be on God's page when it comes to giving people hope for both tomorrow and the issues of today.

Just as our lives can be used by God to draw people to Jesus, the way we live and treat others can repel people from God. In your life right now, are people missing out on God's hope because you aren't fastening your identity steadily on God? Could inconsistency in your identity be the reason those around you refuse to consider that God has a plan?

Jesus is God's all-powerful answer to society's chaos.

I remember when I first met my friend Jocelyn White. She started volunteering at Shepherd Church when I was on staff there as an associate pastor. Even though she had an amazing job dancing for Disneyland, she left that job to work at our church as an assistant to one of our pastors. If you met Jocelyn, you'd quickly realize that she's an incredible leader. It wasn't long before she started overseeing one of our church's multisite campuses.

While working at our church, Jocelyn attended a conference and heard Gary Haugen speak. Gary is an amazing communicator and the CEO and founder of International Justice Mission. He and his team have dedicated their lives to fighting for justice and ending modern-day slavery. Jocelyn's heart was moved and was never the same. She and her husband, Peter, made a commitment to serve God by working to end slavery and helping some of the more than forty-five million slaves alive today.[4] They weren't sure what that would look like, but they knew that God had a plan.

It wasn't long before Jocelyn started working with International Justice Mission, serving alongside the L.A. Metro Task Force on Human Trafficking, and began her own organization called Slavery No More. Today, Jocelyn's platform is growing as she receives opportunities to travel the world, speak in churches and conferences, talk with world leaders, counsel, and more.[5]

Even though Jocelyn wasn't out attacking Christians or people of other faiths, she still reminds me of Saul in Acts 9. Jocelyn, too, had a moment when her heart was awakened and she decided God was calling her to do more than she ever thought she could. She leveraged her relationship with Jesus not only for her own salvation but also to influence and help society around her. Jocelyn realized we should be more concerned about what we can do today rather than fear what will happen tomorrow.

We can do the same. We should leverage the relationship. God has uniquely made you and called you to serve him. How we leverage our relationship with Jesus is going to be different for each of us. I truly believe that God placed a passion in Jocelyn's heart for ending slavery. I have many friends who have dedicated their lives to fostering and adopting children no matter the cost. Not too long ago, I said goodbye to another friend as she headed overseas to live in a country, teach in a school, and tell others about Jesus. I met a couple last year who view their whole purpose in life as being church planters—planting church after church in their city that they love. These people I've mentioned (including Jocelyn) are ordinary people like you and me, but they listened to God. Like Saul, they weren't content to remain sitting in their living rooms when they felt God move in their hearts. No, they got up and charged the hill!

So, how are you going to leverage the relationship? How we leverage our relationship with Jesus to help others is far more serious than we probably care to admit. And it's a serious issue to God as well. God paid a hefty price for Jesus to die on the cross for our sins. Jesus didn't face death so we could sway in and out of a relationship with him, forgetting who we are and ignoring hurting people around us. That is why Saul (later known as Paul) said that those who follow Jesus "should no longer live for themselves but for him who died for them and was raised again." He continued, "So from now on we regard no one from a worldly point of view. Though we once regarded Christ in this way, we do so no longer. Therefore, if anyone is in Christ, the new creation has come: The old has gone, the new is here!" (2 Corinthians 5:15–17).

Since tomorrow belongs to God, we who have a secure relationship with Jesus can graciously offer hope to people today. We'll unpack that more in the upcoming chapters. From here on out, it's going to get a lot more practical—and a lot more personally challenging!

REFLECTION AND DISCUSSION QUESTIONS

1. Read Acts 9:1–31 in one sitting. What are some of the implications of this passage?

2. Has there ever been a time when you had to give someone "tough love"? Why was tough love necessary? Did you handle the situation well?

3. As Saul began persecuting Christians, did he seem to believe he was serving God? Can we reconcile a combative attitude with God's mission? Why or why not?

4. Why do you think we're so quick to judge the motives of others but not our own?

5. Once Ananias and Saul leveraged their relationships with God (trusted him), they began to see lives around them change. How can this be true for you? Where in your life do you need to trust God?

OUT-OF-PLACE PEOPLE ALWAYS HAVE A PLACE WITH GOD.

4

Society Is Like an Emergency Room on New Year's Eve

Where were you when the clock struck midnight and 2016 started? I was in an emergency room. Actually, let me rephrase that: I was in the hallway of the ER with a sick child. Let me explain . . .

The day before New Year's Eve, my nine-year-old son had his tonsils taken out. We thought that the day after his surgery would be easier. We were wrong—so wrong. It began with Joel having severe pain in his stomach. His stomach hurt so much that he couldn't sit up for long before doubling over in pain. At first I thought he was just being melodramatic. I walked him over to his Xbox, but when he dropped his controller and didn't want to play anymore, I knew it was serious. I mean, when a nine-year-old boy doesn't want to play video games, you know something is up!

I rushed him to the closest ER. Being hopeful and naive, I reasoned that the hospital might be less busy than usual, since surely people would rather be at New Year's Eve parties than at the hospital. Again, I was wrong—so wrong.

We walked into the emergency area, only to be greeted by a waiting room filled with sick and hurting people. One man was holding a bucket he had been vomiting in. Another guy was having a coughing fit that never seemed to end. An older lady in the back corner of the room was holding her knee in pain. The security guard in the ER waiting room was engaged in an intense conversation with a gentleman of a different ethnicity (it was obvious there was a language barrier).

Rolling my eyes, I went over to the window and got my son checked in. Joel and I sat in the front of the room and waited for what seemed to be forever. Finally, because the ER was so busy and there were no rooms available, my son was placed in a bed in one of the ER hallways. After an hour in the hospital hallway, Joel started vomiting. The doctors found out he had a bad stomach virus that wasn't related to his tonsillectomy—just a very unfortunate coincidence. As Joel continued to throw up, the scabs in his throat from the tonsillectomy began bleeding down his throat. Because they needed to make sure they had the bleeding under control, we were in the ER hallway for more than six hours that night.

I'm not sure how much time you've spent in an ER hallway, but I can tell you that the longer you're there, the more fascinating things you see. As dire as the situation seemed in the waiting room, the hallway showed far worse situations. Some people in the beds were shouting because they were in pain and it wasn't going away. A couple who were severely injured in a car accident arrived via ambulance. The ER went into a frenzy as nurses and doctors rushed to assess their situations. Close by, a prisoner was in a bed and a deputy was guarding him. The prisoner was bearded and elderly, and he just stared at the ceiling as he lay on the bed. Behind us in the same hallway was an elementary-aged boy who was crying. He, too, had a stomach virus, but that wasn't why he was crying. The boy was sobbing and asking his mom, who was sitting next to him, "Why did Daddy leave? Doesn't he love me anymore? I don't understand." I watched the mom as she curled one arm around his head and with the other hand gently patted his arm.

For many people, New Year's Eve 2015 wasn't filled with parties, laughter, and reminiscing over the past year. It was a sad night. It was a rough night. A couple of the staff seemed overwhelmed at the number of people who needed assistance. Some who I assumed were veteran staff members were focused, moving from one bed to another as they sought to help each patient in the moment. Every now and then some staff members would take needed breaks near the nurses' station and catch up on the lives of their coworkers. That night, the ER was a true mishmash of people.

What I saw there taught me a lesson about society. While some of us are enjoying life, others of us are in pain, troubled, dealing with the unexpected, on hold, or facing lousy prospects. Many people have nowhere to belong.

Christians are supposed to be people who make a place for anyone, even those who don't seem as though they belong somewhere, because God made a place for us.

With such a diverse society—one that will become more diverse tomorrow—how are we to think of people who aren't like us? How are we to react to those who are different from us, especially people who are hurting or don't have a safe foothold in community? How should those of us who follow Jesus view people who are coming from a different journey in life than we are?

I'll tell you. We don't ignore them. Christians are supposed to be people who make a place for anyone, even those who don't seem as though they belong somewhere, because God made a place for us. And he wants all of us to enjoy his tomorrow together. Belonging is not only something we receive but also a gift we should give to others. We don't have to be scared or nervous or isolated if God is passionate about everyone, even individuals who are different from us. His love for people gives us faith and courage to engage anyone, *especially* those who are most at risk and pushed to the sidelines of life.

So far we've looked at the fear that many have of an ever-changing society, the power of God to give us true hope, and how we can engage society because we belong to him. Now, as we start heading into the crowd of society, we need to make sure we're aligned with our view of people. When we consider people, we have all sorts of emotions. Some people we admire, some we love, some we can't stand, and all the rest fall somewhere in between. But to God, everyone matters.

FINDING YOUR VIEW OF SOCIETY

As I've talked about society, I've already said more than once that it is basically people. In other words, that's my "Caleb definition" of *society:* "a group or gathering of people." Some examples of different types of societies, or gatherings of people, include

- those living within the North American continent
- Southern California residents
- Christians in the United States
- Maryland Methodists
- small-business owners
- Star Wars fans
- gamers
- high school teachers
- Alabama therapists
- fans of Nicolas Cage movies
- the few Nickelback fans still around
- the decreasing number of cat lovers

You get the picture.

There are many distinct facets to the concept of society. But when we're talking about society in a larger sense, such as a nation, there are classification systems that some have created to describe how people have been categorized. While such societal categories don't define people, they do paint a picture of what our culture looks like and the values that reside among people. There are some cultural lists that do create negative stereotypes. From personality clashes to the refusal to understand one another to uncomfortable feelings between people, some individuals are left out and have a hard time finding their place in society.

No one likes feeling out of place. Unfortunately, national and religious societies alike have become skilled at making sure people feel that way. Some people don't want to be around those who are different, difficult, or hard for them to understand. Anyone can feel left out or leave others out. Have you seen such examples? Have you and I been such examples?

- If you see someone you presume to be homeless walking toward you, do you cross the street?
- Have you made assumptions about the work ethic of people who are older or younger than you?
- Do you treat your coworkers differently if you discover they're transgendered?
- Does it seem easier to attack or act indifferently toward someone who has a differing opinion on abortion?
- Would you jump to immediate conclusions if you saw a teenager with multiple cuts on her arms?
- Are you ever around patients in a hospital and, even if they aren't contagious, don't want to shake their hands?
- Has there ever been a time when you believed that all wealthy people are greedy?

- Have you ever labeled a person as lazy if his income was low?
- Did you ever make assumptions about a mother's parenting skills when you observed her kids screaming in a department store?
- Was there ever a time when you or someone you know treated a woman in the workplace differently just because she was a woman?

Whether we want to own it or not, all of us have someone or some people who—for whatever reason—make us feel uncomfortable. We allow fear to get the better of us, and it can cause people to do some horrible things to their fellow human beings. As my little green Jedi friend named Yoda says, "Fear is the path to the dark side. Fear leads to anger. Anger leads to hate. Hate leads to suffering."[1] For most of us, our view of society needs a major adjustment.

But how does God view society? When he looks down from heaven at the United States or any nation, what does he think about the people as a whole? Does he think in terms of categories or classes? We need to understand God's view of society. For Christians, the implications of how God views society will affect our view of it. However he feels about something or someone, we should follow suit.

Luckily for us, Jesus provides perspective.

NO ONE LEFT OUT

One day Jesus was at a Pharisee's house for a party and was hanging out with some of the elite of society. They weren't just the elite—they were the *religious* elite who believed they were better than most. If you're not familiar with Jesus and his teachings, here's a quick lesson: he was quick to put people in their place when they thought they were better than others.

While at this party, Jesus painted a picture of how God views society and what it will look like in God's tomorrow. Jesus began his story by saying, "A certain man was preparing a great banquet and invited many guests. At the time of the banquet he sent his servant to tell those who had been invited, 'Come, for everything is now ready'" (Luke 14:16–17).

Here Jesus described a man who obviously was part of the upper class. This man had a house big enough for people to be able to gather for a party, he had a servant, and he had sent out invitations. By the way, this is the kind of party you would want to go to. It would be like getting an invitation to a party put on by the most popular pastor in your town, with the richest people and community leaders expected to be in attendance. Chances are, you wouldn't say no. The response from the invitees, however, is a reason this parable is so astounding: they wouldn't come!

> They all alike began to make excuses. The first said, "I have just
> bought a field, and I must go and see it. Please excuse me."
> Another said, "I have just bought five yoke of oxen, and
> I'm on my way to try them out. Please excuse me."
> Still another said, "I just got married, so I can't come."
> (verses 18–20)

When Jesus listed the excuses, everybody listening would have been shaking his or her head in disbelief. I'm sure when you read these excuses, you thought they were pretty lame. Yet as weak as they sound today, they were even weaker back then. Here's a little free advice: if you invite someone to hang out but he tells you he can't because he must try out his new oxen, he's lying. What it means is, he doesn't like you—not at all!

Probably in a sheepish way, the servant returned to his master to deliver the bad news.

Furious, the master said something that would have made the audience Jesus was speaking to drop their jaws. The master instructed his servant, "Go out quickly into the streets and alleys of the town and bring in the poor, the crippled, the blind and the lame" (verse 21).

Why would jaws have dropped? Because no one from the elite class would ever hang out with the people Jesus described. In so many words, the master told his servant, "I want you to go to the streets and back alleys of the town and invite those who don't have permanent housing. While you're out there, invite those who are told they have little value, those who are hurt, those who can't see, those who are slow to perceive, and even those who have had issues from birth. Yes, invite them, too!"

For the elite listening to this story, Jesus was painting a version of tomorrow that should have made them very uncomfortable—because they were not a part of it! This is a picture of inviting in those who didn't keep all the rules and weren't looked up to in the society of the day.

Many of those who were left out would have jumped at such an invitation. If you don't have a place, it feels great to be given a place! So I think we can assume that when the servant got done with the new round of invitations, most, if not all, RSVP'd yes.

Still, the servant informed the master that there was room for more. The fact that the master had a house the whole town could fit in was mind boggling. No one in Jesus's audience would have ever seen such a big house. It also highlights the foolishness of the first guests' rejection of the invitation.

Now, get ready for this next one, because when Jesus revealed the master's last batch of invitations to his servant, the jaws of those in Jesus's audience would have hit the ground right before they passed out. "Go out to the roads and country lanes and compel them to come in, so that my house will be full" (verse 23).

Why would this invitation have been the most taboo of them all?

Everyone Jesus is telling this parable to would have caught his point. When the master told the servant to go to the roads in the country lanes, he was referring to people who were not citizens of the town. In other words, by extension, Jesus's revelation was that God was going to invite non-Jewish people into his kingdom. This was scandalous for the Jewish religious elite. But it offered hope for many listening at the time or hearing his words afterward—even you and me.

Out-of-place people always have a place with God.

The parable also shows God's heart for people. God wants everyone to be with him in the tomorrow he has created. This includes those in the upper class, if they'll accept his invitation. But God also has a special place in his heart for those who are left out, hurting, wounded, and exiled because of race, health status, gender, and more. God doesn't like people to be without a place. Out-of-place people always have a place with God.

Or in other words, everyone's invited! Anyone you can imagine gets an invitation to this party, which is a metaphor for the kingdom of God—a phrase Jesus and others use to describe the collection of people from all periods of time who have followed the true God. Jesus showed them a snapshot of God's intentionality toward people as he thought about their place in his kingdom.

God refused to divide people up.

God has a house that can fit everyone.

God wants everyone to have a place.

No matter what class or value has been assigned to you by society, when you follow Jesus, you have it made! Those who have a place with God have a very bright tomorrow. God loves society because it is made up of people. How could he not love people? He sent Jesus to die on the cross for people to follow him in order to bring himself glory. God is glorified when those far from him become his followers. There will be a day when all people will bow their knees to God, and we will see the glory of God as we've never seen it before.

There will never be a time when those who follow Jesus will be without a place. God is an expert in giving out-of-place people a place with him. If you feel out of place, then you're actually in a good place because God has a place waiting for you. In God's economy, everyone is equal. Once you're with God, he won't leave or ignore you. Those who follow Jesus will always belong. And whether it's today or sometime in the future, Jesus followers will never lose their seat at God's table.

Remember the God of Tomorrow principle: *Since tomorrow belongs to God, we can graciously offer hope to people today.* We not only *can* offer hope to people today but we *have to* offer hope to people today. You and I need to recognize that God wants us to carry the invitation to everyone, just as in the parable, the servant delivered the master's invitations. When we follow God, even if we've felt out of place, it's our job to begin engaging society by helping out-of-place people find their place with God. After reading this story, we need to own the same truth Jesus wanted his first-century audience to embrace: God has appointed his followers to carry invitations of hope to those in our society who don't have a place with him. He wants us to invite them and let them know that God is in control, he's got a plan, and they're invited to party with him today and tomorrow. Forever.

God Has a Plan for You

One afternoon several years ago, a young lady came to our church office asking to speak with a pastor. The pastor on call that day just happened to be yours truly.

This visitor was a beautiful young woman, yet her eyes were blood-shot and you could see the residue of tears that had rolled down her cheeks. I instantly felt horrible for whatever she was going through, but my attention was divided. You see, I didn't thoroughly explain when I said she was beautiful. She was beautiful and dressed very . . . well . . . she wore platform high heels, a very short miniskirt, and a spaghetti-strap top.

When she showed up at the church, something inside me said, *Caleb, don't handle this one alone.* So I asked Beth and Patricia, a couple of la-dies from the staff, to join me, and we all sat in the conference room with the door shut. Sensing our visitor's need for comfort and warmth, both of the ladies put their arms around her. She began crying all over again. Through sobs and wiping the tears from her face, she told us her story.

This young woman had grown up in the Los Angeles area. She was the youngest of three sisters. Her sisters and parents went to church with her regularly. Her parents encouraged her to work hard in school, get the grades she needed, and then work hard to get a job where she could ad-vance in her chosen career. By her teenage years, she was consumed with the idea that she would one day be an actress.

After high school, she moved out of her home and got an apartment with friends. She started attending audition after audition, but she got nothing. For months she went to different calls for actresses, and they even complimented her acting abilities, but she never got a callback. Be-fore she knew it, she had run out of money. Rather than go back home and hear the "I told you so" lecture from Mom and Dad, she continued to look for a paying gig.

One morning, as she was walking down Hollywood Boulevard on the way to meet a friend for coffee, she noticed a flyer on the sidewalk. She picked it up. The words jumped out at her: "Want to act? Easy money! Assured roles!" Hoping for an audition and the role of a lifetime, she called the phone number on the flyer and was in an audition office that afternoon. But it wasn't the role of a lifetime. Her casting turned out to be the role that she was afraid would last a lifetime.

You've probably guessed it. She had walked into an audition for a porno. She was about to storm out of the office, but before she left the room, they started mentioning money. And it was a lot of money. She had no clue she could make so much money just by doing a couple of flicks a week. Out of fear of what her family would think of the movies she was making, she lied and told them about an acting career that was forming.

Soon one of the movie producers told her she'd make even more money if she stripped on the side while making the movies. She started stripping.

A couple of years had passed between her first movie and the day she met us in the church office conference room. She had fallen into prostitution, had been beaten by men, and was weighed down by guilt from her life choices. "I never thought my life would turn out like this," she told us, crying.

My heart broke for her. When she was growing up, she dreamed of being in the movies—but not those movies. She imagined what her Prince Charming would look and act like, but none of the men she knew were princes or charming. Anger began to fill my mind. I couldn't stand to hear how so many men had taken advantage of her and used her as if her only purpose in life was to please them. I'm sure some of these men had their own daughters, and I couldn't believe they would want another man to treat their daughters like this. But that didn't stop them.

Knowing how to talk to this broken young woman, one of the ladies on staff gave her words of encouragement and assured her that God hadn't given up on her. Beth understood that the girl who had just come from a club needed to know that God loved her very much. While giving her encouragement, Beth quoted Romans 8:1: "There is now no condemnation for those who are in Christ Jesus." Beth went on to assure her that God loved her and wanted to be in relationship with her.

"I'm hopeless," she responded. "There's nothing God could do for me."

Patricia tried to point her to God and his plan for her life when she quoted Proverbs 3:5–6:

> Trust in the LORD with all your heart,
>> and do not lean on your own understanding.
> In all your ways acknowledge him,
>> and he will make straight your paths. (ESV)

The young lady listened, we prayed with her, and around five that afternoon, something incredible happened. I baptized this young lady who chose to believe that God had a plan for her life. *Amazing* is too soft a word to describe what it was like seeing her leave our church after the day was over. When she entered the church, she cried tears of grief, but when she left the church, her tears were filled with hope from the belief that God had a plan for her and wouldn't leave her. Not only was I proud of this young lady, but I was so proud of Beth and Patricia, who believed God had a plan for her just as he did for them.

CARRYING THE INVITATION

We can and should graciously offer hope to people today, no matter who those people are.

In his sovereignty, God has empowered his followers to make a difference in an inconsistent society. He's tasked those of us who follow Jesus with telling as many people as we can about his desire to be in relationship with them. With some of his last words to his followers before he ascended into heaven, Jesus revealed God's plan: "All authority in heaven and on earth has been given to me. Therefore go and make disciples of all nations, baptizing them in the name of the Father and of the Son and of the Holy Spirit, and teaching them to obey everything I have commanded you. And surely I am with you always, to the very end of the age" (Matthew 28:18–20).

Jesus told the disciples that they weren't to stay and just wait for people to come to them. Quite the contrary! Jesus demanded that they *go* and engage *all nations*. For some of the disciples, hearing such a statement might have been troublesome. Why? When Jesus said *all nations,* he meant non-Jewish people, a.k.a. Gentiles.

We also see God's love for all people reflected in Revelation 7:9 when the apostle John got a glimpse of heaven: "After this I looked, and there before me was a great multitude that no one could count, from every nation, tribe, people and language, standing before the throne and before the Lamb." According to what John saw in heaven, tomorrow is for everyone!

Once you follow God through Christ, it's your job to begin engaging society by helping out-of-place people find hope in God.

If all nations will be represented in heaven, there are ramifications you need to consider. Again, realize that God wants you to carry his invitation to everyone, just as the servant in the parable did. Once you follow God through Christ, it's your job to begin engaging society by helping out-of-place people find hope in God.

So, how do we do this? It requires a change in attitude. That's what we're going to look at in the next chapter. Instead of having an attitude that we should protect ourselves and do as little as necessary for others, we should be ready and eager to meet the needs of others, especially people who feel as though they don't have a place. Before I get to that, I want to tell one more story that shows the importance of giving out-of-place people a place.

As a result of the Tim Tebow Foundation, many churches have started a yearly event that intentionally reaches out to the special-needs community. A church where I served called the event A Night to Remember. While a lot of local churches and ministries have their party around prom time, we had ours around the last day of school. We themed it as an end-of-the-year party. The first time we held this event, we weren't sure who or how many people would show up. However, we had more than we expected. Every year since, we have had an increase in the number of people from the special-needs community who attend.

It was really amazing to see the change in those present at our party. Many people volunteered at our Night to Remember. Some were eager to love on our guests. Others, I knew, initially felt awkward to be around people in the special-needs community; simply put, they had never taken the time to get to know the individuals in that community. After one night of volunteering at our party, those same volunteers became the biggest allies of those with special needs.

One of my fondest memories from this party is of a volunteer and friend of mine named Lorraine. She was paired with a guest for the evening and was helping our guest with whatever she needed. Near the end of the night, Lorraine's guest obviously felt she had been treated so well that she looked at Lorraine and said, "Am I a superstar here?"

Lorraine's eyes welled up with tears and she said, "Yes, honey, you sure are."

I get choked up whenever I tell that story, because it's a picture of what God's plan and his tomorrow will look like *all the time.*

REFLECTION AND DISCUSSION QUESTIONS

1. Be as transparent as possible: Is there anyone or any kind of person in society who makes you feel uncomfortable? Why is this?

2. After reading Luke 14:1–14, why do you think Jesus felt the need to tell the parable of the great banquet?

3. As you read verses 15–24, with which group did you see yourself fitting into: the first people invited; the poor, crippled, blind, and lame in the streets and alleys; or those outside the city limits? Why do you feel this way?

4. In the parable, Jesus said God refused to divide people up, has a house that can fit everyone, and actually wants everyone to be with him. Who in your life is out of place and needs to hear that they have a place? How can you help them understand that God made a place for them?

5. Matthew 28:19–20 is not only our mission from God but also a reminder that he wants everyone in his house (all nations). Revelation 7:9 teaches that heaven will be filled with people from every nation, tribe, and language. Take some time and ask God's forgiveness for anyone you have treated or might be treating poorly. Plead with him to give you a heart for all people.

WE DON'T HAVE
TO LIKE EVERYONE,
BUT WE *ARE*
REQUIRED TO
LOVE ANYONE.

5

Developing a Love-Thy-Neighbor Attitude

I need to make a confession. It's not one I'm proud of. I know there's a good chance you will judge me harshly after I share this news—actually, I judge myself. It wasn't until recently that I even felt the courage to own what I did so many years ago. I've noticed that when I tell people about it, they look at me differently, and I feel as though that mistake is attached to my character forever.

Here we go: I saw *Titanic* no fewer than five times when it was released in theaters.

Let me address the first question you might be asking right now: Why did I see this movie that was too long so many times in the movie theater? The first time, I went just to go see the movie. The second time, I took a girl out on a date because she really wanted to see this film. The third time, my dad wanted to see it, so begrudgingly I went with him. The fourth time, I took another girl out on a date (back in the day, I was a playa with mad skillz), and tragically she wanted to see the movie as well. The fifth time, I was with a group of my friends who were going to see it and I didn't want to be by myself, so I went with them.

I don't know why I feel the need to explain myself to you, but I think it might clear the air between us. My behavior at least shows the lengths I was willing to go to for friends or a date!

Can I just say this movie annoys me to no end?

After the *Titanic* sinks, Rose doesn't let Jack get on that big floating piece of door while they are in the ocean. Rose is a diva. There is definitely room for two. Then Jack freezes to death in the water (big shocker there) and Rose seems surprised that he is dead after not being allowed on the door with her. In her grief, she promises to "never let go," but then she proceeds to pry his frozen hand from hers, thereby sending him to a dark, watery grave below.

Following the pleasant send-off she gave Jack, she finds a whistle on a dead body. Despite the fact that she is dying, she miraculously discovers the lung capacity to blow the whistle so she can be saved.

And may we never forget one of the most annoying scenes in cinematic history: old Rose throws a multimillion-dollar jewel in the ocean as if it is worthless. Good grief! No sane person would do that!

While there are many interpretations to the movie's ending, here's mine: old Rose dies. We learn she's being punished for committing some atrocity against humanity that we aren't aware of. How do we know she sinned in such a vile way? Her spirit is banished to the bottom of the ocean to join her possibly imaginary boyfriend, Jack, and all the other people who died in the *Titanic*. When she arrives, the *Titanic* looks new, and all the people who died now clap their hands and throw a party for her, because obviously they've been waiting this whole time for her to die so the party can begin.

See? Annoying and frustrating.

As frustrating as the movie is, the sinking of the real *Titanic* was even more of a frustrating and sad scenario. What many don't think about is the number of lives that were lost and the *way* those people died.

On April 14, 1912, around 11:40 p.m., the *Titanic* hit an iceberg.

Less than three hours later, in the early morning hours of April 15, the *Titanic* sank. Of the more than 2,200 people on board, around 1,500 of them died. A higher percentage of first-class passengers survived than any other class because the first class was prioritized over the other classes of people on the boat. About 38 percent of the first-class passengers died, 59 percent of the second-class passengers died, 75 percent of the third-class passengers died, and 77 percent of the crew died.

Some other breakdowns of the percentages are even worse. For instance, 66 percent of the children in third class died, as opposed to 17 percent of the children from first class. Meanwhile, only 3 percent of the women from first class died, in contrast with 54 percent of the women in third class.[1] Obviously, some people on the *Titanic* were not willing to go to great lengths to help those in need.

I'd like to think that in the hundred-plus years that have passed since the sinking of the *Titanic,* attitudes among different groups in society have improved. Actually, while there has been improvement in some areas, I fear that the basic problem of separation still exists and is still doing much harm.

Our society is more diverse than it ever has been—*far* more diverse in many ways. We see this reflected in an increasing ethnic diversity within the population, evolving perspectives on sexual orientation, the rethinking of gender identity, a decreasing percentage of people who are engaged in their faith, an increase in new philosophies and world religions, and many other factors. If we try to isolate ourselves from society, we come off as considering some people to be less important and we unintentionally repeat the horrid sin of the first class in the *Titanic.* We also refuse to live in reality by not acknowledging where we are as a society and how our communities and ideas will continue to change in the future. How do you think God views that?

As we discussed in the previous chapter, God wants us to provide a place for people to belong. He wants us to tell out-of-place people that he has a place for them, even if they're different from us. But *how* do we do this? How do we not keep people at arm's length? How do we notice, draw near to, and offer help to individuals if they need it? It starts with an attitude change that motivates us to take the initiative by crossing the divide between us and others. The result is that we become neighbors to other people rather than strangers. It starts with *love*. Not only that, it begins with you and me showing people what God's love looks like. We can't sit back and wait for others to show love first or to "deserve" our love.

I'm probably not telling you something you've never heard before. But when we're thinking about tomorrow and the God of tomorrow, we need to consider *whether we're actually living this way*. Sometimes it's not easy to love others, and as any society continues to progress, it can feel even more difficult.

LET'S BE HONEST

Some of my favorite stories about Jesus involve people who underestimated him and tried to checkmate him with their logic. In a way only Jesus could do, he put them in their place and turned the whole scenario into a teaching moment. For me, one particular account of Jesus stands out from the rest:

> On one occasion an expert in the law stood up to test Jesus. "Teacher," he asked, "what must I do to inherit eternal life?"
>
> "What is written in the Law?" he replied. "How do you read it?"
>
> He answered, "'Love the Lord your God with all your heart and with all your soul and with all your strength and with all your mind'; and, 'Love your neighbor as yourself.'"

"You have answered correctly," Jesus replied. "Do this and you will live." (Luke 10:25–28)

This expert, who knew the Hebrew Scriptures inside and out, decided to test Jesus. My opinion is that he wanted to confuse Jesus so his followers would lose faith in him and he posed his question as a dangerous trap. There's a good chance this expert hoped Jesus would respond by equating himself with God, so there would be legal grounds to subject Jesus to capital punishment.

At the same time, the expert's question had to do with his own relation to tomorrow and God. "What must I do to inherit eternal life?" he asked. Let me phrase it another way: *What must I do to be with God forever?*

Jesus responded to his question with a simple verb: *love.*

Loving God and loving our neighbor are inseparable actions.

Considering all the answers the expert might have been expecting, I highly doubt he was expecting Jesus to tell him to love God with everything and love people as he loved himself. Jesus's words also challenge us today to recognize that loving God and loving our neighbor are inseparable actions. We cannot really know or love one without loving the other. Loving God and loving people are two outward manifestations of our saving faith.

It's difficult to love God at times, but it can be overwhelming to love those around us. If I had to choose who was harder to love—God or people—I personally would say people. Some of us will grow a lot in loving others. Some will grow a little in loving others. Many will have no problem loving others—except for those three people over on the other side of the tracks.

Let me amend my statement that it can be overwhelming to love those around us. Loving people isn't only overwhelming; it can be *next to impossible* (depending on who the people are). If we're going to be literal about what Jesus said, we had better ask ourselves if we've ever had neighbors who were hard to love. I know I have.

LOVING PEOPLE ISN'T A THEORY; IT'S AN ATTITUDE

When we really love God as we should, people will come into focus and we'll love them as God says we should. Even after the brilliant answer from Jesus, his questioner still wasn't aligned with his thinking. The expert wasn't done questioning Jesus, but neither was Jesus done leveraging his questions to teach others about how to live out love.

In Luke 10:29, the expert revealed that his attitude had not changed when he asked Jesus, "And who is my neighbor?"

I suppose that right after Jesus heard the question, he shot the expert a little smile. I can imagine Jesus thinking something like *Thank you for asking that question! I was waiting for that!*

Why was the expert's question about the neighbor's identity so important? The expert wanted to be able to determine the value of another person. If he was the one who determined if someone was lovable, then he was never at fault for unkindness or downright harshness. Jesus, however, wouldn't let him get away with this question.

The two laws Jesus quoted (about loving God and people) were laws that Jewish religious scholars held as significant. They were certain of God's identity, but they spent time debating the meaning of the word *neighbor.* Who was their neighbor? Was it a person living next door to them? Did their neighbor reside on the same block or in the same city?

Could it be that the concept of *neighbor* was bigger than what they thought and it included anyone who belonged to Israel?

Nope.

The concept of *neighbor* that Jesus was about to unpack was bigger than they expected—much bigger, with implications for their theology, their view of society, and their engagement with people. Jesus intrigued the expert and onlookers with a story that illustrates the application of what it looks like to love God and people.

He began by saying that a man was walking along a road when he was attacked, severely beaten, and left for dead. People listening to his story would have looked sad because they understood the context of his story. The particular road Jesus was talking about ran between Jerusalem and Samaria. It was dangerous. People often got mugged and even killed along this road.

The story continues as Jesus said that a priest happened to be walking down the road and saw the beaten man but chose not to help him. Next, a Levite (another person with a priestly role) walked down the road, saw the bloodied traveler on the ground, and chose not to help as he walked on the other side of the road.

By now the shock value Jesus wanted was probably beginning to set in. The people would have gasped at the thought of a priest and Levite refusing to help someone in need. After all, these were two men who were spiritual leaders and set the example for others. Those you'd think would do anything to help did everything to stay away.

The shock value rose even more when Jesus introduced the third character of the story.

A Samaritan, as he traveled, came where the man was; and when he saw him, he took pity on him. He went to him and bandaged his wounds, pouring on oil and wine. Then he put the man on his own donkey, brought him to an inn and took care of him. The next day he took out two denarii and gave them to the innkeeper. "Look after him," he said, "and when I return, I will reimburse you for any extra expense you may have." (verses 33–35)

This had to have come as a surprise to the expert and the others listening. First-century Jewish people couldn't stand the Samaritans. Centuries earlier, when Israel split into two kingdoms, the forefathers of the Samaritans went with the northern kingdom (Israel), while the forefathers of the Jewish people went to the southern kingdom (Judah). The forefathers of the Samaritans married non-Jewish people who hadn't converted to Judaism, and this practice wasn't allowed by God. They also changed some of their theology. Because of all this, for many Jewish people of Jesus's day, it was easier to make all Samaritans into villains rather than get to know them.

> **Jesus shows us the right question to ask: "To whom can I be a neighbor?"**

Nevertheless, Jesus didn't give them time to stew about his characterization of the Samaritan in his story. He quickly drove his principle home.

[Jesus asked,] "Which of these three do you think was a neighbor to the man who fell into the hands of robbers?"

The expert in the law replied, "The one who had mercy on him."

Jesus told him, "Go and do likewise." (verses 36–37)

Jesus's point here is all too obvious. The expert's original question—"And who is my neighbor?"—was the wrong question to ask. Jesus shows us the right question to ask: "To whom can I be a neighbor?"

How to Love Like a Samaritan

To be a neighbor, we need to adopt the attitude of the Samaritan. We must develop a *love-thy-neighbor attitude.* This kind of attitude is crucial for people who trust God more than they fear tomorrow. They're ready to be a part of God's plan to change our world. People apply this attitude in a positive way by helping those in need so that they have hope for tomorrow.

In looking at the parable of the good Samaritan, I believe there are three takeaways that will help us apply a love-thy-neighbor attitude. Want that kind of attitude? Here's how to start.

Meet the Needs of Others So It Is Easier for Them to See God

Helping people reach a place of health (whether physical or emotional) can assist them in achieving a mind-set where it becomes easier for them to consider God. Let's look at what the Samaritan in the story did.

As we just discussed, many first-century Jews would have perceived the Samaritan as a person with little value. However, this Samaritan of "little value" was keeping the two great laws (love God and love people) that the two Jewish characters who worked for God weren't keeping. He had an attitude of being ready to jump in and help anybody in need.

- He didn't know if the wounded guy was important or not, and he didn't care.
- He was concerned about the hurting person and cared for him.

- He valued the hurting man more than his own schedule.
- He had blood and dirt on his clothes, but it wasn't a big deal to him.
- He risked possible disease by helping.
- He valued the man's healing more than the cost of oil, wine, and bandages.
- He allowed the man to ride on his donkey, which means he might have walked.
- He paid for the man's room and needs.
- He extended the offer to cover any extra costs the man might incur.

The Samaritan went out of his way and put himself at risk to make a difference. The two men may have been of different ethnicities, but it didn't matter to the Samaritan. He could love God by helping a hurting person, thereby loving his neighbor as himself. I'm pretty sure that if the Samaritan man had been hurt, after regaining consciousness he would have done everything in his power to get medical treatment. He treated another person with just the same care and concern as he would himself.

I've always speculated about what happened when the Samaritan returned to the inn. I imagine that if the wounded man was still there, he was probably grateful and emotional. If he was Jewish, the ethnicity of his helper probably mattered less to him than it would have before. When the Samaritan returned and struck up a conversation, the wounded man probably hung on his every word because he was listening to the man who had nothing to gain from helping him and yet helped him anyway. Whatever the Samaritan wanted to say to the wounded man carried more weight after he helped him.

For you and me, this example means we should do whatever we can to meet the needs of people around us so we can make it easier for them to see God moving in their lives. For you that might mean listening to a coworker cry about her last breakup even though everything in you wants to run from the conversation. It could be that it's time for you to gather your family or your church small group for service at a shelter that serves your local community. For the people who are served by shelters, each warm night and each meal could be another step toward them accepting God's invitation of hope. Maybe it's as close as home. Your child has procrastinated on an assignment, and despite your threats not to help at the last minute, you conclude that an act of service in this moment might allow him to experience the kindness of God.

I'm not sure what this looks like for you, but there are people all around you who have needs that you can meet. In doing so, you can help them see God.

Refuse the Temptation to Be Unloving—You Don't Have That Right

Jesus quoted two commands, found in Deuteronomy 6:5 and Leviticus 19:18, when he said that tomorrow belongs to those who love God and people. Without hesitation, the good Samaritan obeyed these two Old Testament commands, refused to think of himself first, and had an awesome attitude. He even got down to the level of the beaten man as he picked him up off the ground. When you read the passage, his responses seem almost automatic.

We, too, are under a command from God to love. First John 4:20–21 says, "Whoever does not love their brother and sister, whom they have seen, cannot love God, whom they have not seen. And he has given us this command: Anyone who loves God must also love their brother and sister."

When we decided to give Jesus our lives and follow him, we gave up our rights to not love others. Now, this doesn't mean we don't set boundaries when people have really hurt us. Aside from extreme relational situations, we don't have to like everyone, but we *are* required to love anyone.

It's part of our faith to have a love-thy-neighbor attitude. Those of us who identify as Christians don't have permission to be unkind, rude, harsh, cruel, cynical, indifferent, and so on. Following Jesus means his death on the cross holds us accountable to love God and people. If loving God and loving people are inseparable, how audacious are we to try to separate them? What amount of arrogance do we display when we try to put a filter on the word *neighbor*?

> **We don't have to like everyone, but we *are* required to love anyone.**

Loving your neighbor has *no* filter.

The expert learned that if he removed his filter from how he thought of love, he could be a neighbor to anyone, and anyone could be a neighbor to him. *Of course!* we might think. More often than not, we mock first century people who couldn't see that point. We could have reasons why we think we're further along than they were and don't have as many prejudices.

Oh, really? Is our society truly *that* advanced in ethical thought? My two cents: I think not. We never know when God will put people in front of us who need hope. In addition, we really don't know how we'd respond to the people we don't like if they're the ones needing our assistance.

If you saw a Muslim being bullied, what would you do? Well, if *you yourself* were being bullied, you'd try to stop the situation. Should you help the Muslim who's being hurt? Yes, and not just because God would want you to but because you'd do it for yourself.

Whenever you see an apparently homeless person asking for food, how should you respond? Imagine what it might feel like to be in that situation. If you were, would you be hoping and maybe even praying to God to bring food? If so, then serve the homeless person in the way you'd serve yourself or want to be served.

Simple: Make a Decision to Act

More than once, I've heard my friend Josh Ross say, "The church has not been called to be the protectors of the establishment, but to be a force for hope in the world."[2] The best way to develop a love-thy-neighbor attitude is to *act*. While people love to learn and understand new concepts, the consumer mind-set of American Christians has kept us in more Bible studies and Christian bubbles and less engagement with those far from God. The seventeenth-century clergyman William Gurnall saw this same danger in his time when he said, "Knowledge may make thee a scholar, but not a saint; orthodox, but not gracious."[3] I love learning, studying, and diving into the endless depths that are the very study of the true God. But I don't believe that God grants me knowledge to fuel my arrogance or to further mask my hypocritical mind-set. He gives me insight and awareness of himself to further my mission here: to help people follow Jesus to the glory of God.

Love is never indifferent.

If we as believers who make up the church want to graciously offer hope to people today, we must be authentic and care about others. There are those who view church as being mainly about them, but they will never get much out of it or put much into it. As Dietrich Bonhoeffer once said, "The church is the church only when it exists for others."[4]

Love requires action. Love is never indifferent. Love always makes a difference.

AUNT DIANE

My wife's aunt Diane is an amazing woman with a strong faith in God. Actually, she's not really her aunt; she's a good friend of the family.

Diane and her husband couldn't have kids. They tried to have children, but after multiple doctor appointments, they realized they would never be parents to biological children. While this is tough on anyone, it was especially tough on Diane.

One day she was working in the ER and was helping a young woman who had come in with a shoulder injury. After performing a routine urine test, Diane brought the results back to her and informed her that she was pregnant. With tears in her eyes, the young woman told Diane that her husband would probably want her to get an abortion. They were living with their two sons in a trailer behind Union Station in East LA. To the young woman, the thought of adding a third child to their situation was overwhelming, but she didn't want to have an abortion.

Aunt Diane didn't want her to have one either. After listening to the young woman's worries, Aunt Diane finally had her chance to speak. "What if I told you that there was another choice? You can have the baby and put the child up for adoption."

The young woman replied, "I would only do that if I knew for sure that the child would be placed in a loving home."

With a smile, Aunt Diane asked, "What if I could guarantee you that home?"

Aunt Diane then made the young woman a deal: if you have the baby, I'll adopt the baby. She agreed, and nearly nine months later Aunt Diane was a mommy.

Having a love-thy-neighbor attitude is a command from the Lord, something we should work on and live out for others' good. It's also a change we can make that can bring rich blessing to ourselves, sometimes in ways we would never have expected, as Aunt Diane discovered! Opening ourselves to relationship offers rewards that self-protection could never give.

REFLECTION AND DISCUSSION QUESTIONS

1. How have you seen our society label and categorize people? Have you personally ever done anything to try to address this problem?

2. In Luke 10:25, a religious expert asked a question that implies he thought his standing with God was based on what he did for God. Why do you think it's so easy for us to believe that God is impressed when we keep the rules?

3. Read Luke 10:26–29. Do you think "To whom can I be a neighbor?" is a better question than "Who is my neighbor?" Why or why not?

4. Make a list of how the Samaritan was a good neighbor to the man who was wounded. What can you personally learn from this list?

5. After reflecting on the parable, in what ways do you think love is an attitude and action more than it is a theory? What can you do to ensure that love is a primary attitude in your life?

YOU MIGHT NOT
BE ABLE TO
WALK A MILE IN
ANOTHER
PERSON'S SHOES,
BUT YOU CAN GET
A PICTURE OF
HIS JOURNEY.

6

For Relationship, Start Here

Our family is filled with Disney freaks. I love so many things about Disneyland: the experiences, the food, Star Wars, Marvel, the rides, the creativity, the smell of food that fills the air, the positive music you hear throughout the park, the smiles from kids, laughing at parents who carry their sound-asleep kids out of the park at night (because I've been there), and many other reasons that would take up too much space in this chapter.

What I really admire about Disneyland is that the people who work there know what they value, and one of their primary values is the guest experience. When you're a guest there, you can be assured that the cast members (staff) have gone through significant training on guest relations. They value your experience so much that they will do just about anything to make sure you'll return.

On one of our Disneyland outings, we saw an older gentleman fall on the ground in front of the Haunted Mansion. He wasn't seriously injured—he just lost his footing. I was walking over to help him when, out of nowhere, Disneyland cast members arrived on the scene. I still have no idea how they just appeared. The cast members immediately formed a circle around the man so he wouldn't be bothered or stepped on by the crowd.

When I saw that, I thought, *What kind of place would have ten of their employees respond immediately to a person's minor fall by encircling him until he was ready to get up?* I'll tell you what kind of place: a place that knows what's important to the organization.

I love what Walt Disney's nephew Roy once said of his father, Roy, in a Disney stockholders meeting: "My Dad was quoted once as saying, 'It's easy to make decisions, once you know what your values are.'"[1]

I'm blown away by Disneyland's knowledge and ownership of its values. It doesn't take long for guests to see that this organization values *people.* The Disneyland cast members are willing to go to great lengths to make sure their customers have a fun and magical experience.

On the other hand, I'm underwhelmed by the knowledge, conviction, and action pertaining to values in our society. I've never been accused of being a pessimist (quite the opposite, actually), but I don't think humanity's natural inclination is to value the interests of others. On the contrary, I assume that most people must work at valuing others. With certain people, I know I must do this. If everyone decided to really work at valuing one another—regardless of status or ethnicity—our society would look better. Maybe fewer families would break apart. I bet drug trafficking might be a tragedy of the past instead of a current reality. Social media would be more encouraging than discouraging. Quality education and care would be available for people, regardless of their location. Violence and mass shootings would come to an end.

Some people try to deal with the glaring horror of such offenses by making speeches without action, telling jokes that lack concern, ignoring reality altogether, or putting too much trust in earthly political parties that have their own agendas. Instead of considering the implications of society's problems, we give our attention to other things.

But let's not forget what we learned in the previous chapter: God wants us to develop a love-thy-neighbor attitude because he loves people. Why else would he send us out in boldness and graciousness to offer hope to those around us? If people are valued in the Magic Kingdom, how much more are they to be valued in the kingdom of God?

If people are valued in the Magic Kingdom, how much more are they to be valued in the kingdom of God?

Back in chapter 1, I told you how it's all about relationship. This is where we start engaging society—by interacting with other people in one-on-one relationships. You know, good old-fashioned friendships, or at least kindly acquaintanceships. So let's start with the idea that people actually matter. They matter to God because he made them and loves them. In the same way, they should matter to us as well.

I've got a few simple truths to share with you about getting to know people and treating them as if they're valuable. The first is starting with an attitude of humility about yourself. If we want relationships, we can't hold ourselves aloof from others, and we certainly can't put ourselves above them either. Why would we?

WE'RE ALL ON THE STRUGGLE BUS

Have you ever spent time reading about Jesus's family history?

It's not exactly perfect.

Checking out Matthew 1:1–17, we find some of these less-than-perfect people. Judah slept with his daughter-in-law, and that's icky, right? Rahab is on that list, and she was a prostitute. David is also on the list, and while he was a good king in many ways, he also committed adultery and murder. You don't become Church Member of the Year for what he did. David's son Solomon wasn't any better. He was a serial adulterer and drew away from God. In the next generation, Solomon's son Rehoboam split the kingdom. Then, on down the family tree, another king named Manasseh was one of the most violent kings ever.

Those are just a few of the skeletons in Jesus's family closet. I'm not sure about you, but if I had family like that, I wouldn't want everyone to know about it. Fact is, though, there are no perfect families in the Bible. There aren't even any perfect individuals in the Bible (other than Jesus, for obvious reasons). Every well-known figure in biblical history made mistakes. Every. Single. One.

- Adam threw his wife under the bus as soon as God started interrogating him (Genesis 3:8–12).
- Cain killed Abel (Genesis 4:1–8).
- Noah got drunk (Genesis 9:21).
- Abraham gave his wife away . . . twice (Genesis 12:13–15; 20:2).
- Sarah asked Abraham to sleep with her servant (Genesis 16:1–2).
- Lot got drunk and slept with his daughters (Genesis 19:32–36).
- Isaac and Rebekah each showed favoritism toward their sons (Genesis 25:28).
- Isaac gave his wife away (Genesis 26:7).
- Jacob betrayed his brother, lied, and had multiple wives (Genesis 27:18–30; 29:21–30:24).
- Jacob's sons murdered people, sold their brother into slavery, and slept around (Genesis 34; 37:12–28; 38:1–18).
- Moses murdered a man and was also prideful (Exodus 2:12; Numbers 20:1–12).
- Aaron's sons were self-centered and dishonoring (Leviticus 10:1–3).

- Eli's and Samuel's sons were out of control (1 Samuel 2:12–17; 8:1–5).
- David's father didn't think very much of him (1 Samuel 16:8–11).
- Saul manipulated his daughter to marry David (1 Samuel 18:17–30).
- Hosea's wife was a prostitute (Hosea 1:2; 3:1–3).
- Jesus's brothers didn't believe in him until after the Resurrection (John 7:1–5).

And this brings us only up to the time of the Christian church.

Why did God include all these stories of broken families in the Bible? Perhaps he simply wanted to show off his power. If God is powerful enough to use the people in that list, how much more can he use you and me? If God can redeem the people on that list (those who submitted to him), how much more can he redeem you and me and that person we think is so far off base? It could also be that God wishes to reassure us that, no matter what, he is working all things out for his good. If God could use all these people for his greater purpose—bringing Jesus into the world—how much more is he using us to bring about the fulfillment of his plan? That's a tomorrow we can all look forward to!

On the other hand, what if God's main reasoning for including the tales of imperfect leaders and broken families is to remind us that we're imperfect and broken too? How in the world will we be able to positively influence people in society if we don't remember that we're wounded and hurting ourselves? Why would we even think we have any chance of giving people hope for God's tomorrow when we can't even show them the hope that is transforming our lives today?

When you meet people in society whose lives are out of balance, remember that apart from God's grace, you are no different! (Even with grace, you've still got your problems, right? Remember the toxin of sin in the human soul.) We're all on the struggle bus in life. We've got problems. We have needs. So that gives us a commonality and lets us talk to others on the same level.

We can connect with people—no matter how different they are from us—on the level of our broken humanity. And that leads me to the next part of treating people as though they matter (which they do): listening to them.

THE MAGIC OF LISTENING

I'm not the first to put it this way, but perhaps God gave us two ears and one mouth for a reason. Maybe we should listen more to where others are coming from.

What I'm talking about here is *empathy*. Well-known author and speaker Brené Brown said that empathy is "feeling with people."[2] What a simple and concise definition! Empathy isn't necessarily about trying to make people feel better, but feeling *with* them.

My friend Reggie Joiner added some commentary to Brené Brown's definition. Reggie said empathy is "to pause your thoughts and feelings long enough to engage with the thoughts and feelings of another person."[3] I like his definition as well, and quite honestly I wish it described more of how I operated. Sometimes when someone is in a place of despair and shares his story with me, I'm tempted to immediately tell about a time when I was hurting in a similar way. Before I know it, the whole conversation has become about me. Just so you know (and I'm sure you do), none of that is helpful. What *does* add value to another person is the willingness to be fully present with him and refuse to make anything about yourself.

If we truly care for people, we need to listen to them as best we can.

Why? Because listening leads to empathizing with others. The more we empathize, the more we can understand their emotions, know where they are, and hear their hearts. Even though we might not agree with certain people, that doesn't mean we treat their perspectives lightly. Empathizing isn't the surrender of our personal beliefs or a compromise of orthodox theology. Rather, empathy emphasizes the value of other people. It doesn't mean we have to have all the answers or even completely comprehend the situation we're learning about. It does mean you and I need to be fully present in the life of a particular person. You might not be able to walk a mile in another person's shoes, but you can get a picture of his journey.

You might not be able to walk a mile in another person's shoes, but you can get a picture of his journey.

One time I heard Reggie Joiner give clarity as to how deeply Jesus valued empathy. He was preaching on Matthew 5:38–48 and got to verse 41: "If anyone forces you to go one mile, go with them two miles." Reggie said, "Mile one fulfilled an obligation. Mile two changed the nature of their relationship." He then asked, "What changes when we go the second mile for someone?"[4] Wow!

Author and pastor Louie Giglio encourages us to consider that "simply by our proximity to Jesus, we can bring hope and life to people and places trapped in discouragement and despair."[5] Do Giglio's words sound familiar? If so, maybe it's because he was echoing some more words from Jesus's most famous sermon: "You are the light of the world. A town built on a hill cannot be hidden. Neither do people light a lamp and put it under a bowl. Instead they put it on its stand, and it gives light to everyone in the house. In the same way, let your light shine before others, that they may see your good deeds and glorify your Father in heaven" (verses 14–16).

Our society needs Jesus followers who carry the invitation of God with a love-thy-neighbor attitude. Whether people know it or not, they need us to engage and relate more than anything else. They're counting on us to believe that since tomorrow belongs to God, we can graciously offer hope to people today.

Near the beginning of Donald Trump's presidency, he signed an executive order that banned refugees and people from several Muslim nations from entering the United States for ninety days. Needless to say (maybe you remember), there was a lot of debate on the ethics of such an order. Some agreed 100 percent with President Trump; some regarded his order as the word of a dictator who would control America.

One of the most irritating parts of this scenario was what some of President Trump's supporters said. From words on social media to videos to blogs, some lumped every single refugee into a category of Muslim extremists who wanted to destroy America. While there may have been some terrorists who could have been stopped from entering, the majority were innocent men, women, and children. Many of these families were fleeing brutal and difficult situations.

Clustering everyone together in one group is wrong.

Refusing to understand where others are coming from is wrong.

Ignoring what families and individuals must go through is wrong.

When you listen and see beyond yourself, you can empathize. But this raises the question of what we do when others start saying stuff we think is way off base. It will inevitably happen, and usually very soon in our conversations.

PRICELESS LOVE

So, how do we process our disagreement and friction with people while we strive to love and support them? I believe love relies on acceptance, not agreement.

If this principle sounds familiar to you, it may be because you read my previous book, *Messy Grace,* where I discuss some similar principles. From what people have told me, this principle has been one of the most helpful parts of that book, and I return to it here because it's crucial guidance for how we engage people in a rapidly changing society. We accept others as individuals who are valuable to God and valuable to us, without agreeing with any beliefs or actions that violate the standards of God.

Love relies on acceptance, not agreement.

When we have family or friends who make life choices outside what we see as God's boundaries, it's much easier to just go along with their decisions. The problem with going along with them is that we've based our love for those people on our agreement with them. Such love is shaky and will be short lived at best. Eventually, we'll find something we don't agree on, and then what? Will the one or many issues we agree on be enough to keep our relationships with them? One way or another, our love for those people will expire.

Basing your love for other people on acceptance is much better. Acceptance means that you might not agree with them on everything but you choose to accept them regardless of agreement. In other words, accepting them means you love them for who they are (and who they are not) and where they are, no matter what. Acceptance means loving them as they are, while agreement is about supporting decisions in their lives. My love for others is found in my acceptance of them and not my agreement with them.

It's completely possible and appropriate to be in a relationship with someone and not agree with the decisions he or she makes. Look at how Jesus lived this idea out in his life:

- Jesus accepted Peter but didn't approve of his racism, which Paul eventually confronted him on (Galatians 2:11–16).
- Jesus loved John and James but didn't affirm their violent tendencies (Luke 9:54–55).
- Jesus didn't write off a legalistic Pharisee named Nicodemus, but he didn't support a theology Nicodemus had that wasn't honoring to God (John 3:1–21).
- Jesus was willing to value an outcast Samaritan woman by speaking with her, giving her hope, and refusing to affirm a history of harmful relationship choices (John 4:1–42).
- Jesus willingly accepted an invitation to Zacchaeus's house, but when he agreed with Zacchaeus's confession, he was also agreeing that his previous practices were wrong (Luke 19:1–10).

In my own life I feel and have felt this tension. In high school I got invited to a Bible study and tried to disprove Christ but instead became a Christian and felt called to preach. I also changed my view on sexuality to what I hold today: God created sexual intimacy to be expressed in marriage between one man and one woman. At the same time, I learned that a theological conviction is never to be a catalyst to devalue another person.

When I came out as a Christian to my parents, they kicked me out for a while. Eventually I lived with them again, but in a new reality. I lived in the tension of accepting parents I dearly loved without theologically agreeing with their choice to be in same-sex relationships. While there were tense days between us, I learned so much more about who they were and how I was called to relate to them:

- My parents had been hurt deeply by some Christians.
- They thought God hated them.
- My actions toward them and their friends deeply influenced their view of God.
- The theology that shaped my view on marriage was the same theology that called me to relentlessly love my parents.
- While I wasn't called to beat them over the head with my beliefs, I could have confidence to engage in discussion when God led.
- My parents respected my faith, even though we disagreed, because I was fully present in their lives.
- God loved my parents immensely more than I did.
- I wasn't supposed to "fix" my parents but instead point them to the God who loved them.
- Despite the rallying cry of some people, not all who disagree over life choices are causing harm to the other person in the relationship.

Through this journey, I discovered that when it comes to my parents and others, love relies on acceptance, not agreement. Though our journey isn't over, my parents eventually submitted their lives to Christ.

Not every story has such an ending. Attempting to have a love-thy-neighbor attitude by living in the tension of acceptance and agreement with someone is not easy. Hear me on this: if I had chosen to see *acceptance* and *agreement* as synonyms, I'm not sure my parents would have submitted their lives to Christ. If I really believed there was no difference between accepting and agreeing with my parents, we probably wouldn't be in a relationship today.

Love relies on acceptance, never agreement. Cheap love is based merely on agreement. Don't settle for this. Even in some of my closest relationships we'll disagree, but I refuse to abandon the relationship. Pursue priceless love that accepts people (no matter who or where they are) with the understanding that while you can't "fix" them, God can. Love that is based on acceptance instead of agreement can reunite relationships, heal families, save lives, and even change eternal destinations.

An Unusual Lunch

Just so we're on the same page, how do we value people?

- Put yourself on the same level as others, because we're all imperfect and needy.
- Listen empathetically as they tell their stories.
- Accept them as people even when you must disagree with some of the things they say or do.

Look, it's not really all that hard to show other people they matter to you. But it's revolutionary because this is the way you start to form real relationships with others who are different from you. It may be that it'll help them start to form real relationships (or better relationships) with God, too.

All of us probably know someone with whom we could begin this kind of relationship. Try to think of somebody you know who is different from you and with whom you could initiate a friendly conversation. As the conversation gets started, do me a favor: just listen. Look for that place inside of you where you can relate with this person's hurt, and just listen from that place. Don't try to fix her reality; instead, join her reality. Keep your eyes focused on her. Make a choice to really hear her story. Acknowledge what she's going through and ask a simple question: "How can I help?" Maybe remind her, "I'm in your corner" or "I'm with you" or "I'm so sorry." Trust me—this engagement will make more of a difference than trying to make your conversation with her the one-stop shop for fixing her.

No one has taught me the power of empathy like Tami and Jill.

Whenever I preach at a church, I like to go to the lobby area afterward and meet people who attended the service. At one of the churches where I spoke, two ladies in their twenties named Tami and Jill came up to introduce themselves. Tami was about my height with short dark hair, a ball cap worn backward, and a pleasant smile. Jill had long brunette hair and a soft voice. They told me how cool it was to find a church like this one.

I shared with them that I agreed—that I thought highly of this particular church as well.

They went on to ask questions about the worship services and what the doctrinal statement was. I tried to answer them as best I knew how, and then Tami got to her main question: "Jill and I are a couple. Honestly, we just want to know if this is a church that will walk with us while we're journeying through this."

"Let's get together and chat after this next service," I offered. "I'd like to hear your stories." They left, cautiously excited.

Not long after I finished the final service, I found myself sitting at a restaurant across from Tami and Jill.

"Can you both tell me your stories?" I asked them after we ordered our food. "I want to hear where you've been in life and how you got here."

For the next thirty minutes, I intensely listened to what life was like for these two young ladies. People's stories always shock me. The journeys of Tami and Jill were no exception. By the time they were finished, I was on the verge of tears. Happy memories were paired with pain, but it was primarily the pain that was expressed as they shared their life experiences with me. In their pursuit of God, they had been kicked out of churches and scoffed at by their Christian friends. When Tami was finished with her story, I thought to myself, *If I were her, I'd hate men. Honestly, I would hate men and wouldn't trust them at all.*

"So, what's your story?" Tami asked.

Little did they know! It was their turn to sit in shock as I described my story to them, all about growing up with two gay parents.

When I was done, Jill was ready with her first question: "What do you think of us?"

Tami added on to that, "I know you probably don't agree with our choice to be in a relationship—we get that. But do you think we could attend the church where you just preached?"

My friend was the pastor of this church, so I felt very comfortable in answering for him. "Anyone is welcome to walk through those church doors," I responded. "And you're right—both the church leadership and I definitely have different perspectives on sexuality based on our theological convictions. However, my biblical beliefs don't allow me to mistreat anyone."

I assured them they would be loved at this church and asked if they were okay attending, knowing there would be a different theological stance on relationships. I also wanted to know if they were ready to experience tension between their beliefs about relationships and the convictions they'd hear in sermons. (I guess for all of us, there's tension of some sort between how we live and what's preached during the services.)

At this, tears welled up in Tami's eyes. She had come to a pivotal moment in life where she saw that not every church that held a differing doctrinal belief would hand her a negative label. Watching her in this conversation made it all worthwhile. While we must be honest about God's truth, I'm convinced that we need to give space for people to sit in rows and gather in circles so they can begin to be open to embracing God's grace. After all, spiritual heart surgery is a process and takes time. Removing idols from our hearts to make room for God is a delicate process. Someone gave me the chance to sit in rows and gather in circles. Even though my salvation was instantaneous, it took time for me to come to the point where I submitted my life to Christ. Growing in faith is a process, and we should allow others to experience it in order for the gospel to fully grasp their hearts.

When we choose to empathize with others, they feel heard and loved. People who feel that way often are more open to what God wants to do in their hearts. As their hearts open, they will be more likely to be receptive to a faith that can carry them into tomorrow's hope.

REFLECTION AND DISCUSSION QUESTIONS

1. Read Matthew 1:1–17. The people on that list all made big mistakes. With whom can you most identify and why?

2. Both Brené Brown and Reggie Joiner have their own definitions of *empathy*. Take some time to write your personal definition of it. Do you live out your own definition that you've created? How have you seen yourself grow to be more or less empathetic?

3. Why is love based on acceptance more powerful than love based on agreement? Have you or someone you know experienced both kinds of love? How did each one make you feel?

4. How does it feel to know that God is completely satisfied with you in Christ—that no matter what, he won't love you less or more? Reflect on this truth some more and say a prayer of thanks to God that he's with you regardless of your mistakes and others' opinions of you.

5. Think of a person in your life right now who's hurting. Consider how he would feel if you were fully present with him in the moment? How would he feel if you put your phone away, looked him in the eye, listened, acknowledged his pain, and committed to be "in his corner"? Now go and do that for someone.

IF GOD'S KINDNESS LEADS PEOPLE TO REPENTANCE, SHOULDN'T MY KINDNESS LEAD PEOPLE TO GOD?

7

Impersonating
the Oppressed

"I feel oppressed," the young man said as my jaw dropped. I couldn't believe what he was saying. Before I continue, let me give you the backstory.

After speaking at a conference earlier in the day, I was having coffee with a young man in his early twenties. He had reached out to me the week before the conference and wanted my opinion on a personal matter. It turns out he had recently told his politically ultraconservative parents that he was in a same-sex relationship and hoped they would fully agree with him. I bet you guessed it—they didn't. From what he told me, however, his parents seemed to want to keep their relationship with him. Sure, things were tense, but after processing what he told them, they didn't throw him out of the house, continued paying for his graduate school and car insurance, bought him clothes, and showed him in so many other ways that they loved him, despite their disagreement with his decision to be in a same-sex relationship.

"How does that make you feel?" I asked him, expecting him to brag about his parents.

"Not good," he said. "Actually, I feel oppressed."

My jaw dropped. "Oppressed?" I asked, hoping I had heard him wrong.

"Yes, I feel oppressed!" he said loudly. Some of the people in the coffee shop looked at him when he raised his voice. I shrank back in my chair so they wouldn't assume I was the one oppressing him.

"They don't agree with my relationship and that triggers me—they're oppressing me." This time he said it a little quieter.

"And what do you want from me?" I asked him. "How can I help in this situation?"

He paused, leaned forward in his chair, and said, "I want to know if you agree with me—that I'm being oppressed."

Without missing a beat, I said, "No, I don't."

Sometimes I lose my filter. It doesn't take much for me to express my thoughts without first considering what I'm saying. I've found that depending on the circumstances, this trait can be a help or a hindrance.

"I'm sure you're a good guy, but you're being a brat," I continued. He looked at me as if I were crazy, so I responded to his facial expression. "Yeah, you're being a brat," I repeated. "Have you seen oppressed people? I have. I've seen them in Third World countries. I've seen my friends experience oppression in the form of racism. I've seen my parents experience it by the way they were treated. I've seen oppression."

The look on his face hadn't changed, so I kept talking. "How do you have the audacity to claim oppression when you're a white, middle-class, twentysomething graduate student with skinny jeans, money to attend a conference, and an internship at a successful corporation? How can you cry oppression when your parents are processing your news, still love you, have kept you living in their house, and are paying for graduate school? How? Just because they don't agree with your life choice to be in a same-sex relationship? That's not oppression; that's disagreement."

Even though I felt sad for this young man, I was also angry. The frustration I felt came from my realization that we've come to a point in our society where we equate respect with agreement. I don't care if they have a liberal or conservative worldview, so many people will claim to be tolerant until there's disagreement between them and others. Our understanding of words such as *tolerance* and *oppression* is lacking. As various divides grow deeper in our society, the heat also increases with those with whom we disagree.

I want to acknowledge that there are people we all know (possibly you) who have actually experienced oppression and been victimized. When I hear the word *oppression,* I think of people forced into slavery by extremists, those who have limited rights based on their ethnicity or other facets of who they are, orphans forced into unhealthy homes, prisoners in prison camps, and individuals who experience physical, emotional, verbal, or any other kind of abuse. These are just a few examples of oppression; there are many more.

Lately, though, an increasing number of individuals are choosing to deal with cultural tensions by falsely labeling themselves as oppressed. Erroneously wearing this title leads to a victimhood mentality. The young man I was having coffee with was a perfect example of this. Playing the role of the victim allowed him to take revenge in a passive-aggressive way. I'm not sure if he meant to have this attitude or not, but he had adopted it, and it was hurting him more than anyone else.

Christians who live in false victimhood are shortchanging the gospel.

In previous chapters we've discussed the importance of cultivating new relationships and investing in those around us. We've highlighted the importance of having relationships with people who are different from us, hold opposing ideologies, or even make us feel uncomfortable. There's one thing that can easily derail these potential relationships. It's doing what the young man in the coffee shop was doing: manufacturing or exaggerating the harm others have done to us. What a way to lose credibility and shut down conversation!

If you're a Christian, I hope you'll consider not playing the victim or shouting oppression when it's not true. Christians who live in false victimhood are shortchanging the gospel. To better engage society, you and I need to adopt the God of Tomorrow principle: *Since tomorrow belongs to God, we can graciously offer hope to people today.* How can we offer hope to others if we manufacture victimhood and live as if there's no hope? We can't. If we do, we compromise the influence we could have on those around us (especially those who are hurting). To put it more bluntly, having a victimhood mentality slows down God's message of love that we should deliver to society.

Here's another painful consequence of falsely living as a victim: not only will people know we're hypocrites (claiming to follow Jesus but living without hope), but they'll also probably figure out that we're being less than transparent. If the people around you know you're a Christian and hear your lies about oppression, what will they think about God? Individuals who work with you, live near you, and do life with you might even develop a sour view of Christianity (if they don't already have one). As you process the continual changes in society, strive to be accurate about problems and pain. Refuse to fabricate your circumstances to your own benefit. Ditching distorted oppression talk is a way to ensure graciousness as we offer hope to people today. If you try to offer hope to someone who really is being oppressed (abused, hurt, and so on) and falsely claim that you're oppressed, the other person will soon discover your tactic. I'd be willing to bet that such an experience will push them farther from God than they were before.

Strangely enough, when we wear the oppression badge inappropriately, the consequences and pain we bring upon ourselves make us our own oppressor!

Now, you may say this isn't a problem for you—that you wouldn't dream of claiming oppression falsely. You certainly may be right about your intentions. But take a moment before dismissing the possibility to consider some other ways a defensive and bitter attitude might manifest itself. For instance, do you ever maintain that others have robbed you of the good life you once enjoyed? When was the last time you threw someone else under the bus to protect yourself, even though you shared some of the blame? If you have a bad day, do you ever make the decision to leverage those bad experiences to get special treatment from others?

Real victims exist. You might be one of them. Still, more than we'd like to admit, it's probably easier for us to play the victim card. I've found that one of the most common ways of falling into this mentality is bemoaning the loss of a supposedly better time.

THE MYTH OF THE GOOD OL' DAYS

Each time we have an election, I hear phrases such as these from people in both main political parties:

- "Let's go back to the good ol' days."
- "Things are really bad right now and they're getting worse."
- "I remember when things used to be better in this country."

I understand what people mean when they say these phrases. There was a season in their lives—whether during their childhood or after childhood—when life seemed to be going well, or as best as could be expected. Those were the good ol' days. It doesn't take much for that feeling to change. A particular law that goes into effect, a new leader elected to office, or even a new supervisor coming on board their organization can bring that season to a sudden halt. Stuck in a new reality, they think of the past season as the good ol' days.

Even in Christianity, we see the good ol' days mentality at play. For some progressive or theologically liberal Christians, the good ol' days might refer to what America was like under a previous presidential administration or congressional majority. To give some examples, many would view the broad availability of health care, marriage equality, and more as a step forward in the rights of many Americans. The thought of how a Republican president could reverse or damage such policies might strike fear in the hearts of those who wouldn't vote for him. At the same time, some conservative Christians and evangelicals frequently talk about how they live in a society that's vastly different from what they grew up in. Issues such as legalized marijuana, abortion on demand, the shrinking of freedom of religion, or new perspectives on the definition of marriage make them long for the world they experienced before these were topics of conversation.

I want to ask people, regardless of their political affiliation, "What good ol' days are you referring to?" Really, when were they so good?

Some might point back to the "good ol' days" of the eighties, seventies, sixties, fifties, or some other decade. Obviously, this would vary depending on those you're talking to. I personally don't think it gets better than the music and movies of the eighties—that's as close to heaven as we're going to get!

Others will say the "good ol' days" are the *Leave It to Beaver* and *Ozzie and Harriet* days. Those were the days when people understood what family was. Now, there are some solid principles from those days that we could benefit from getting back to. But still I must ask, *Really? Are those the good ol' days?* The irony is that America had the "ideal family" handed to them on TV night after night by whom? Hollywood—the very community that some Christians constantly criticize now!

But even back then, could everyone relate to those "good ol' days"? They might have been the best of days for a few of you, but for someone else, they were the worst of days. Could Latino or African American families relate to *Leave It to Beaver* and *The Adventures of Ozzie and Harriet*? Could Korean families? Interracial families? Single-parent families in which the mom had to work several low-paying jobs in the extremely male-dominated society of fifty years ago? Could those in orphanages relate? What about families wounded by extreme racial discrimination of the fifties, sixties, and beyond—could they relate? All the kids who suffered abuse from trusted loved ones probably couldn't relate either—or feel comfortable sharing about the abuse with others. And I imagine that wives being beaten by their husbands couldn't relate to the perfect Mr. Cleaver.

Let's not forget families who couldn't live up to the "exemplary family" model even if they wanted to. While an expectation was created (perhaps unintentionally) of what family should look like, feelings of guilt and shame might have fallen on those who weren't able to reflect the image. It was rare that a child at that time would feel comfortable sharing her same-sex attraction with her mom and dad.

Hollywood realized that the model televised family ideal failed. So, what was their response? Hollywood has swung the pendulum all the way to the other side. Now anything goes, from reality TV shows such as *Sister Wives* to the glorification of families that relate to each other in toxic ways, such as those seen on *The Real Housewives of* _____ (fill in the blank with whatever city or state you choose).

This new vision of families is far from desirable—really far. But we have to be careful not to let it skew our memories of the past. The televised family ideal in decades past had wholesome elements, but it wasn't completely Christian, nor was it relatable to many people.

Or let's consider politics and society. Were the good ol' days when a conservative wasn't in the White House and abortion rights weren't in question? Were the good ol' days when abortion was more accessible and the government overtly funded organizations such as Planned Parenthood to the point where we've aborted millions of babies in our country?[1] Were those the good ol' days? No one has ever really been able to nail down for me when the good ol' days were.

Personally, I believe that since the fall of humanity, there's been no such thing as "the good ol' days" (except for the resurrection of Jesus and the birth of the church in Acts 2). Bemoaning the loss of some mythical golden age is a way of complaining that others have done us wrong. By blaming society for changes that we perceive to be harmful, could we be implying that others have oppressed us? The kind of society we thought we had, and expected to continue to have, appears to have been taken away from us.

The case of "the boy who cried oppression" that I told about at the beginning of this chapter is an obvious example of the victim mentality. Sometimes, though, this attitude manifests itself more subtly. Certainly, I suspect, it's more widespread than many of us would admit. This mentality hurts all of us, and that's why we'd better look for a good example of how to deal with it.

A BETTER ALTERNATIVE TO THE VICTIM MENTALITY

In the fall of 2016, the University of Chicago mailed welcome letters to the incoming class of 2020. One section of the letter read as follows: "Our commitment to academic freedom means that we do not support so-called 'trigger warnings,' we do not cancel invited speakers because their topics might prove controversial, and we do not condone the creation of intellectual 'safe spaces' where individuals can retreat from ideas and perspectives at odds with their own."[2]

Good for the University of Chicago for taking this stand!

And bad for society! The very fact that the University of Chicago had to issue such a statement tells us where we're at, socially.

Refusing to go along with the trend of oversensitivity is a starting place. It might surprise you, but Jesus himself goes much further than that. He says that his followers shouldn't play the victim or seek to get revenge in any way *even when we really have been injured.* This is contrary to what society suggests we do when we think someone has done us wrong. You know, *Amp up the drama! Play it for sympathy! Turn the situation to your advantage!*

Jesus offers a better way. His way is all about a response that has the potential to not just let free speech go on, as the University of Chicago is trying to do, but actually change a relationship.

In Matthew 5:46, we're challenged by Jesus's words: "If you love those who love you, what reward will you get?" So Jesus tells us to love those who treat us poorly? Yes, he does, especially in Luke 6:27–29: "Love your enemies, do good to those who hate you, bless those who curse you, pray for those who mistreat you. If someone slaps you on one cheek, turn to them the other also. If someone takes your coat, do not withhold your shirt from them." In a similar way Jesus also reminds us to imitate God's posture toward others "because [God] is kind to the ungrateful and wicked. Be merciful, just as your Father is merciful" (verses 35–36).

Every time I read those verses, I get convicted.

Jesus spoke those words when the Jewish people were under the oppression of a brutal occupying force, unlike anything I face. You don't face such a thing either (at least not if you're an American, as I am). I think Jesus could have said, "Hey, everyone, you have no idea what these guys are going to do to me. I'm the Son of God, and I'm going to let them beat me and kill me. Can you believe what I'm going to have to go through?" Would that have helped us put our situation in perspective?

I also notice that Jesus didn't say, "Be merciful, just as your Father is merciful—unless others mistreat you. In that case, leverage their treatment of you to gain sympathy and attention from others." Nope, Jesus didn't say that, either.

If God's kindness leads people to repentance, shouldn't my kindness lead people to God?

Several years later, under the same imperial regime, Paul asked Roman Christians to reflect God's example in loving those who make life choices that lead to sin: "Don't you see how wonderfully kind, tolerant, and patient God is with you? Does this mean nothing to you? Can't you see that his kindness is intended to turn you from your sin?" (Romans 2:4, NLT). I can't help but wonder that if God's kindness leads people to repentance, shouldn't my kindness lead people to God? If Paul was able to write this verse under the inspiration of the Holy Spirit in a society that was far from God and continually moving farther away, how much more should I be kind and gracious toward others?

Never once in all of Paul's writings did he encourage people to feel sorry for themselves or act like martyrs. However, later in the same book, Paul echoed the words of Jesus:

> Do not repay anyone evil for evil. Be careful to do what is
> right in the eyes of everyone. If it is possible, as far as it
> depends on you, live at peace with everyone. Do not take
> revenge, my dear friends, but leave room for God's wrath,
> for it is written: "It is mine to avenge; I will repay," says the
> Lord. On the contrary:

"If your enemy is hungry, feed him;
      if he is thirsty, give him something to drink.
   In doing this, you will heap burning coals on his head."

Do not be overcome by evil, but overcome evil with good.
(12:17–21)

I love what Paul said here. Don't repay evil. Do what you can to have peace. Don't take revenge. Fight evil with good.

So, while we aren't responsible for how others treat us, we are accountable for how we treat them. God holds us responsible for how we react emotionally. Let that sink in for a moment—that's deep stuff right there! Kindness is a choice to act like God when everything in us tells us we shouldn't.

Kindness focuses on love.

Kindness replaces negativity with joy.

Kindness helps us relate to others.

Kindness grows relationships.

Kindness fosters spiritual maturity.

Kindness grants inner peace.

Kindness allows us to step out of the way.

Kindness acknowledges God's sovereignty.

In the face of disagreement, anger, and pain, kindness isn't the most attractive sell for us. Rather than consider differing thoughts, it becomes much easier to just read, watch, and listen to those who agree with us (even if they're edgy and only mostly agree with us). As comfortable as that response might feel in the moment, it could carry long-lasting consequences that will devastate people in the future, and that's not the kind of tomorrow God wants to offer anyone.

PLAYING THE VICTIM IS TOO PRICEY

In the movie *The Hobbit,* Gandalf says, "Saruman [a wizard who goes to the dark side] believes that it is only great power that can hold evil in check. But that is not what I have found. I've found it is the small things, everyday deeds of ordinary folk that keeps the darkness at bay. Simple acts of kindness and love."[3]

Kindness, love, mercy, forgiveness, blessing. These are the qualities God expects of us when others mistreat us. This approach is the opposite of crying oppression. It's not about getting an advantage for ourselves when we are (or perceive ourselves to be) mistreated; it's about getting an advantage *for the other.*

Crazy, eh? Not fair? Nope. Costly? Yes. Worth it? For sure!

In my own life I've learned that the short-term cost of doing good outweighs the long-term cost of taking matters into our own hands. If we continue to exaggerate and fraudulently portray ourselves as oppressed, we add to the chaos of society. Our contribution to society's chaos might be displayed as

- confusion as to who is and isn't oppressed
- less transparency
- a lack of critical thinking
- the growing absence of empathy and the increased devaluing of others
- more people believing that God is irrelevant

Here's another way to look at it: manufacturing oppression destroys empathy.

We do so much damage to society and ourselves when we misuse the concept of oppression and make our plight sound worse than it is. Whether we're oppressed or not, everyone experiences pain. And to some degree, many of us carry pain with us. Although pain is relative to the individual who experiences it, all pain is *not* equal to individuals. Different kinds of pain deliver a variety of consequences. I've noticed that most people who are enduring significant amounts of pain don't scream it from the rooftops.

As I pointed out earlier, when you lie or exaggerate about pain, you'll eventually get exposed. People will reason that if you truly carry the oppression you claim, you should have a greater capacity to handle difficult circumstances. It always seems as if the ones who talk so much about their oppression are unprepared for the storms of life—that's usually a dead giveaway for me. It's not that people who have endured or are enduring pain don't struggle in each season or have their dark moments, because they do. However, even in the dark moments, these people embody a strength and maturity that is seldom found in others.

Love Is Never Manufactured

Near the end of my conversation with the young man in the coffee shop, we began talking about acceptance. "You don't understand: I don't feel loved," he said, battling my plea for him to grasp his parents' love. "If they loved me, they would be on board with this."

"They do love you," I shot back, "and while they aren't on board with this life choice to be in a same-sex relationship, they are on board with you as their son."

And I wasn't done yet. "You need to be concerned more with your attitude than theirs," I challenged him. "Think back to the way Dr. Martin Luther King Jr. related with those who opposed him. He responded in love, not physical violence or emotional indifference."

"Some of us still need to be aggressive," he said with a half smile that almost seemed to say *Gotcha!*

I ended the conversation shortly after that. There was no way we were going to be on the same page. He was looking to build a coalition of people who agreed with him so he could feel better about using a word like *oppression*.

If God loves everyone, then that grants us the strength to love anyone.

Real love is empowered by God, who loves everyone. If God loves everyone, then that grants us the strength to love anyone. Love takes time, empathy, and discovery of who others are. It's the result of intentional investment in other people. The power to love anyone flows from our relationship with God. The kind of authentic love I'm speaking of isn't manipulated, tricked, exaggerated, manufactured, or forced by anyone. It can't be.

I'm not sure about you, but anytime I've tried to build a coalition of people who agree with me (so I can feel better about a situation), it has never resulted in the kind of love God possesses. Gathering a group of supporters might work if you're running a campaign for office or lobbying for a bill to be passed, but it falls short in personal relationships. If people are forced to feel something, they might align their feelings with you for a while to avoid disagreement. But eventually they'll stop siding with you, because forced emotions aren't authentic emotions. Ignore the temptation to control others' emotions by misusing words such as *oppress* or *victim*. Their feelings won't last, and your relationships with them will be horrible on the other side.

While fake oppression isn't an issue for most people, there is an issue that can cause numbness in all our hearts. In the next chapter, you and I are going to tackle this significant and dangerous issue that has hindered Christians from engaging society with graciousness. Let's unpack *indifference*.

REFLECTION AND DISCUSSION QUESTIONS

1. Has there been a time when you or someone you know played the victim? Did people eventually see through the performance?

2. What were the "good ol' days" for you? What made them good? Were those days good for everyone?

3. Read Luke 6:27–36 and Romans 2:4. What does God say about our kindness? How seriously does he take our treatment of others?

4. According to Romans 12:9–18, how does God say we should live out a life of kindness? List all the different examples Paul uses in this passage.

5. When we exaggerate our pain, what will the eventual result be? Why is kindness a better option than false claims of oppression?

IT DOESN'T MATTER
HOW MUCH YOU
KNOW IF YOU
HAVE NO
COMPASSION
TO SHOW.

8

The Injustice of Indifference

Every four years brings the Summer Olympics to the world. I love the Olympics. I'll stay up late and watch various events. Seriously, there is no other time during those four years when I'll stay glued to the TV watching gymnastics. The 2016 Olympics were special for me because my friend Cody Jones competed in the Paralympics (throwing the javelin). He was amazing.

The stories of those who trained so hard and overcame unbelievable odds to compete in the Olympics are inspiring. The Olympics point us to the possibility of all countries uniting and working together. The theme of unity is highlighted not only within a team's national pride but also through the unity of nations joining and working together.

What breaks my heart about the Olympics is that while we're witnessing the unity of humanity, the underbelly of humanity also appears. It's ridiculous that at a world event with so many good qualities, the opposite is also present. Drugs are prevalent at the Olympics. Human trafficking escalates in whichever city the games are being held. While the world celebrates nations coming together, people are hurt and taken advantage of. It's sick and disgusting. Rarely do people know the evil that happens at the Olympics and other such events. Sometimes I wonder, *If people really knew, would they care?* When I mention this, I'm not trying to make you or anyone else feel guilty. I'm revealing a fear I have about the present state of society.

I'm concerned that as we see the erosion of morals and ethics in society, we'll also witness the diminishment of human value. In other words, I see society becoming *indifferent* toward the hurt and pain of others. I know many people would argue with me and say that we've made great strides toward human rights and the promotion of healthy ethics. I agree and applaud such efforts. We should pat ourselves on the backs for those advancements, but let's acknowledge that we still ignore some of the greatest tragedies of our society. Poverty, lack of medication, unemployment, greed, and more continue to dominate the path of too many people.

This is a reality we can't afford to ignore. When we discount injustice, we prove ourselves to be indifferent. Our awareness of the oppression that others face is paramount. Injustice is real and happening all the time. In many cases, people who aren't following Jesus are taking the lead in fighting it. That's way out of balance. Christians shouldn't be indifferent bystanders when it comes to opposing injustice; we're meant to be out in front leading the war against it! Some are already doing this. More of us ought to be.

True, we might not always agree with others on what constitutes injustice or the best way of defeating it. But our disagreements on what is or isn't injustice shouldn't stop us from doing our part to battle it.

Our God hates injustice. The Old and New Testament agree fully on this. We're reminded of this truth when we read verses such as Isaiah 58:6:

> Is not this the kind of fasting I have chosen:
> to loose the chains of injustice
>   and untie the cords of the yoke,
> to set the oppressed free
>   and break every yoke?

In similar fashion, Jesus read the following passage in what was probably his childhood synagogue:

> The Spirit of the Lord is on me,
>> because he has anointed me
>> to proclaim good news to the poor.
> He has sent me to proclaim freedom for the prisoners
>> and recovery of sight for the blind,
> to set the oppressed free,
>> to proclaim the year of the Lord's favor. (Luke 4:18–19; see
>>> Isaiah 61:1–2; 58:6)

To God, every single person matters. God hates injustice because it demeans the value he assigned to those he created. How can you and I be indifferent toward people who are experiencing something God hates? I believe when people are rescued from injustice, they have a greater capacity to believe that God offers them hope. Remember, hope is part of the God of Tomorrow principle: *Since tomorrow belongs to God, we can graciously offer hope to people today.* May we have the courage to offer hope by combating injustice.

Perhaps the first injustice we must fight is our own indifference.

Perhaps the first injustice we must fight is our own indifference. Think about it for a second: indifference toward injustice is injustice itself. Indifference toward people God loves is indifference toward God. As we're about to see, God takes injustice seriously, but he takes our indifference toward suffering people *very seriously.*

WHEN GOATS GET IN THE WAY

In Matthew 25 Jesus told a parable that serves as a metaphor for events that will occur at his return. But mainly it shows how our treatment of those who are suffering reveals our faith. The backdrop for Jesus's parable is a first-century shepherd who had to tell the difference between his sheep and the goats that would wander into his fold. Some biblical scholars say it was difficult to distinguish between a sheep and a goat. But a good shepherd would know his sheep. If he still struggled to discern which was a sheep or a goat, the shepherd could cut some of the animal's hair. A goat's hair would always feel different from that of a sheep.

As Jesus began this parable, he positioned the sheep to represent those following God and the goats to represent those not following God. In the story, Jesus says that at his return, he will separate the sheep from the goats by putting the sheep on his right and the goats on his left. The right-hand seat was a place of honor, much like when someone calls "shotgun" when getting in a car. But the right-hand seat was more than just bragging rights; it meant you were aligned with what was important to the king. This is where you would find the sheep—animals that had immense value for the wool and meat they provided.

Jesus tells the "sheep" that they can enjoy their reward with him because they fed him when he was hungry, gave him drinks, invited him in, and basically served him. The "sheep" then ask him about his claim of serving him. "Lord, when did we see you hungry and feed you, or thirsty and give you something to drink? When did we see you a stranger and invite you in, or needing clothes and clothe you? When did we see you sick or in prison and go to visit you?" (verses 37–39).

Jesus's reply in verse 40 is haunting and still holds us accountable today: "Truly I tell you, whatever you did for one of the least of these brothers and sisters of mine, you did for me."

We learn from the parable that when someone helped a suffering individual who lived under the king's oversight, he or she was actually helping the king. The person who was in need meant a lot to the king, and the king was touched when that individual was loved. In other words, Jesus takes it personally when we help those who are in need, because God is passionate about people.

The world and everything in it was created to honor God. You and I were created to honor God. There's a manifestation of peace when God is at the center of our thoughts, ambitions, actions, and engagement of others. As much as we might desire justice and peace, God desires justice and peace even more. He takes it personally when we ignore those who don't have justice or peace. Thus, in the parable when Jesus has interactions with the "goats," he's extremely tough on them. Whereas he tells the "sheep" that they served him by serving others, he tells the "goats" that they ignored him by being indifferent toward others. Jesus places such indifference on the same level as the pride of the devil by assigning the indifferent "goats" to join the devil and his fallen angels in eternal fire.

Confused, the "goats" want to know when they ignored him.

Jesus answers them, "Truly I tell you, whatever you did not do for one of the least of these, you did not do for me" (verse 45).

The upshot for the "goats"? "They will go away to eternal punishment" (verse 46). Meanwhile, the "sheep" receive "eternal life."

Now, hear me out on this. In no way, shape, or form is this passage saying that you must *do something* to be saved. Rather, it speaks to our lives after the moment of our salvation. It's what the brother of Jesus wrote in James 2:18: "Show me your faith without deeds, and I will show you my faith by my deeds." Those who love God don't just have beliefs—they have actions. Their beliefs are lived out in their actions, and their actions reveal their beliefs.

CHALLENGING THE NARROW MINDED
AND HARD HEARTED

My wife's name is Amy. If you met her, you'd be blown away by how beautiful she is. You'd also find yourself thinking, *What in the world is she doing with Caleb?* Believe me, I ask myself that same question every day! She's tall with dark hair, deep brown eyes, and a smile that could light up any room. You might be surprised to discover, however, that she's Mexican. Far from what some stereotype Mexicans as, Amy is usually fair skinned (though she can tan when she wants). Her family has more of a Spaniard background. She majored in Spanish in college, spent a semester studying in Spain, and even taught middle school and high school Spanish for a year at a Christian school.

The unfortunate part of not looking Mexican is that she has often been around others in conversation when racial slurs are shared. Amy has found herself in situations in which some people air their true feelings about Mexicans because they don't see any dark-skinned Hispanic people around. She's heard Mexicans described as

- lazy
- incompetent
- trying to steal our jobs
- violent offenders

While there are individuals of every ethnicity who are lazy, incompetent, and violent, it's not fair to describe one group of people as such. Making the most of such a conversation, Amy has been quick to share that she's Mexican, that her grandparents came into the United States legally, and that her family have been hard workers and have contributed to society. Most people backpedal on their comments when she confronts them. I enjoy being around her when she is correcting such ignorance. It's truly fulfilling to watch verbal injustice confronted and weak worldviews challenged.

Still, it's been disheartening when she's been around people who have shown how bigoted they are. I wish I could tell you otherwise, but she's heard some Christians lower themselves enough to say things such as, "Send them out of the country!" or "Put all of them in jail!"

Indifference extinguishes any compassion we might have toward others.

Where's the compassion? Where's the concern? Where's the biblical worldview that God created all and that everyone counts? Indifference extinguishes any compassion we might have toward others. Actually, I believe that indifference toward anyone eventually allows the dismissal of everyone. Indifference falsely gives people permission to determine the value of any one person. Indifference is injustice.

HOW TO SAY GOODBYE TO INDIFFERENCE

I like how the New Living Translation renders what Paul said in 1 Corinthians 4:20: "The Kingdom of God is not just a lot of talk; it is living by God's power."

The journey to tomorrow isn't just a lot of talk—it's compassion and action. We've got some work to do, because if we are going to fight indifference and injustice, we must have compassion. We must really believe that everyone counts, because if we don't believe that, why should we do anything?

Learn to Despise Injustice

Even though I've said it before, let me say this as clearly and bluntly as I can: God hates injustice. We should too.

In January 2014, former basketball star Dennis Rodman made a controversial visit to North Korea.

Why?

For the birthday of the North Korean leader Kim Jong Un, Rodman brought a group of former NBA basketball players to play a special basketball game. Later, Rodman revealed his deeper intention for the trip. "It's about trying to connect two countries together in the world, to let people know that: Do you know what? Not every country in the world is that bad, especially North Korea."[1]

As well intentioned as Dennis Rodman's trip and comments may have been, I must disagree with his opinion of North Korea. While the people of the country might not be "that bad," the leadership of that country certainly *is*.

The North Korean government has been the facilitator of countless injustices, such as carrying out brutal beatings and awful forms of execution, permitting the horrible mistreatment of women, putting people in concentration-type prison camps, allowing people to starve, pursuing nuclear weapons, and more.

Yes, Dennis, it actually is "that bad."

This example is just one of various countries, governments, regimes, and factions that oppress their people. Christians cannot take such injustice lying down. Those of us who bear the name of Jesus follower are compelled to stand for justice and represent those who are powerless. We have a biblical mandate to call out injustice and hatred, because love is never indifferent.

And while we are loving and gracious, we must let our voices be heard amid injustice. How we act today determines what society will look like tomorrow. If we see but don't speak out or act against suffering and wrongs, we must ask ourselves if we really believe that God is in control.

The poet Ella Wheeler Wilcox wrote,

To sin by silence, when we should protest,
    Makes cowards out of men.[2]

When we choose not to be part of the solution, we not only demonstrate a shaky view of God's control of tomorrow but also live as cowards.

Ask God to give you opportunities to speak up for the right values. Use social media, letters to your government leaders, personal conversations, and other outlets to let your courageous voice be heard. Communicate your convictions on peace, life, safety, family, wise handling of money, and so on. God used the words of many people in the Bible to encourage, teach, and bring accountability to government leaders and citizens of countries; he can use you, too.

Allow Your Heart to Break

God cares about people. His heart is yearning to be in relationship with the people around you who make up society. Make sure your heart is echoing what's on God's heart.

In August 2016, I was attending Willow Creek's Global Leadership Summit. Many of the conference speakers challenged me in different ways, but none more than Melinda Gates. If I think too much about her session, it keeps me up at night. She was being interviewed by Bill Hybels and was talking about her work to help those who are hurting in the world. She and her husband, Bill Gates, give enormous amounts of money away to charities and causes that will save lives. But one comment she made struck me and will forever stay with me: "If you want to make a difference, you have to let your heart break."

Wow.

But we don't like to let our hearts break, do we? You know why? Because breaking hearts *hurt*! We don't like to hurt. However, if we don't allow our hearts to break, we will never find the passion to do something to help those whom no one else is helping.

When your heart breaks, it isn't a sign of weakness—it's a virtue of strength. President Dwight Eisenhower once said, "History does not long entrust the care of freedom to the weak or the timid."[3] The strength, boldness, and passion come only when we're first touched in the heart.

Ask God for a Mission

Journalist Priscilla Alvarez described a young American woman who started out with a normal life—until everything changed at the age of seventeen. Her mother went to prison because of embezzlement. She found comfort in the words of a man she met online, so she bought a bus ticket and traveled to see him. She was surprised to find that he was much older than she had thought. And far from being the kind and compassionate person he had presented himself as online, he told her that if she stayed with him, she would have to "earn her keep." Alvarez wrote, "For four days, she said, she worked for him by going to an area for commercial sex. Soon after, another pimp approached her, promising to fill a void—family."[4]

This young woman eventually left to go back home, but she fell into another relationship with a different pimp. Thankfully, she got out of the industry because of people who were committed to helping women trying to escape human trafficking. The people who helped this young woman weren't content to just sit on the sidelines and watch others drift away in the negative undercurrent of society; they did something about their concern.

While we cannot be involved in each cause, we can choose one or two causes to champion. If we choose just one area of injustice to help, our laser focus will make more of a difference than a scattergun approach to many causes. For you, that might be a cause in your local community, assisting a missionary overseas, partnering with your church and focusing on a particular country to share the love of God with, learning about a justice mission organization, and so on. Don't just give money to an organization—get involved in your local church. Serve at a local organization that helps people in need. It could be that the person you're living next door to is in a rough situation and just needs someone to show compassion. Maybe it's the person who's in class with you or works in the office across from you. Everyone else avoids her and she is a little odd, but she needs help.

Not a Shred of Indifference

The more I watch the news, the more indifferent I feel when I see horrible things happening. Of course I notice when an awful event happens on our soil. We all do. My heart hurts when I hear of multiple bombings in a foreign country, a new dictator rising to power, sermons and speeches on sex slavery, or a growing number of children who are homeless, but a few minutes later I'm back into my own world. Even though I don't mean to be, I can be indifferent.

God takes my indifference personally because just as love is never indifferent, so God is never indifferent. There's not a shred of indifference in him! He is completely good. When it comes to people, God is passionately committed to those who follow him and to helping others see the importance of following him. He promises help for today and a hope for a better tomorrow to those who follow him.

God takes our indifference toward "the least of these" very seriously because he identifies with people. He created people and purposed them.

It doesn't matter how much you know if you have no compassion to show.

It doesn't matter how much you know if you have no compassion to show. God is concerned about the wrongs that we're mostly concerned about but then lose track of. He's passionate about the injustice that we never hear about and the people who are enduring painful lives that we'll never know. It's time for us to build some concern by really believing that everyone counts.

REFLECTION AND DISCUSSION QUESTIONS

1. What do you believe is the greatest injustice of our time? Why do you believe this to be true?

2. Read Isaiah 58:6; 61:1–2 and Luke 4:18–19. How does God define injustice, and how does he address it?

3. In Matthew 25:40, 45, Jesus told people that what they "did" or "did not do" for others is what they "did" or "did not do" for him. What does this mean, and how is this possible?

4. "It doesn't matter how much you know if you have no compassion to show." Do you agree with this statement? Why or why not?

5. What injustice are you passionate about? For what cause are you convicted to take a stand? Before you create a plan to take action on a cause, look at the Bible to see what God has to say about this cause. Pray and ask for his blessing on your endeavor.

WHATEVER LEADERS DO WHILE THEY HAVE AUTHORITY, GOD BRINGS GOOD OUT OF THE GOOD AND EVEN GOOD OUT OF THE BAD.

9

Making Tomorrow Great Again

Without question, for many Americans the most frustrating presidential election took place in 2016. Hillary Clinton obtained the Democratic nomination for president but seemed to lack the momentum Barack Obama and Bill Clinton had. To the chagrin of many, Donald Trump became the Republican nominee for president. While Trump was riding a wave of excitement in his followers, he lacked the support of many key leaders in the Republican Party.

Both candidates had potential strengths they could bring to 1600 Pennsylvania Avenue, but their opponents and the press highlighted their weaknesses. For instance, trust was one of the negative issues for Hillary Clinton that became a recurring theme throughout the campaign. Emails were leaked revealing that the leaders of the DNC had decided there was no way they could allow Clinton's Democratic primary opponent, Bernie Sanders, to be nominated. When followers of Sanders discovered the bias, some disengaged from the DNC. Later, thousands upon thousands of government emails were discovered on Clinton's private server. To make matters worse, some of them were classified. The FBI investigated, and while it found evidence of carelessness, it recommended that the attorney general not prosecute Clinton. A few days before the election, more emails were discovered. The FBI director made Congress aware of it, and the press latched on to the story. For many, the prospect of breaking the glass ceiling with the first female president was exciting, but could she be trusted?

Donald Trump's impulsive words were one of the weaknesses he and his team had to deal with the most. While he was a man of great business experience, he struggled to control his speech in tense situations and behind closed doors. Throughout his campaign, comments he made about Latinos, celebrities, immigrants, women, ideologies, and more began leaking out to the press. A well-known example was a recording of Trump making extremely lewd comments regarding a woman he wanted to spend time with (and if you remember, that's putting it delicately). The press and social media alike had a field day with that recording. Christian leaders came out of the woodwork to let people know they were not supporting Trump. There were many who had to decide if his comments reflected what he really believed.

These are just two examples of the negativity that dominated the 2016 election.

In the end, despite many riots, angry social media statuses, furious blogs, and bewildered conversations, Donald Trump was elected the forty-fifth president of the United States.

I remember this election well, and I'm willing to bet you do too. People asked me repeatedly, "How did we get to the point where these two people are our choices for president?"

It's a great question, and I believe that the 2016 election was ultimately a reflection of our society. For quite some time, when one looked at the two primary American political parties, there was a lack of teamwork on the part of some leaders. Because of the influence of some politicians, the parties began to work together less and strive more to ensure their party became the ruling party, no matter the cost. As a result, when one party controlled the White House, the Senate, or the House of Representatives, some members of the opposing party would work tirelessly to undermine their actions. As the years went on, the positions of some in each party grew more and more extreme, until we were presented with a two-party system that brought forth what many people see as one of the most extreme elections in US history.

> **Extremists in any community never lead anyone to unity and peace.**

While some reading this might not consider Hillary Clinton or President Trump extremists, I think we can all agree on one thing: extremists in any community never lead anyone to unity and peace.

It raises a good question: When the political landscape of tomorrow feels bleak at best, how do we handle our disagreement with our leaders? Some of us are so fearful of tomorrow that, however unintentionally, we allow our fear to give us permission to treat our leaders poorly. But God has never allowed us to dishonor any leader. Yes, we need to get involved in fighting injustice and the wrongs we see in society. We also must remember that we are supposed to continue to honor those in leadership.

A TALE OF A REALLY, REALLY, REALLY BAD LEADER

When we read the New Testament, we find that the writers said little about the politics of the Roman Empire. What they said when they did refer to the Roman government might astonish us, as it did their first-century readers.

For instance, Jesus was once asked if Jewish people should pay their taxes to Rome (the empire that occupied their land, killed their people, and was led by a pagan dictator). What was Jesus's response? "Give back to Caesar what is Caesar's, and to God what is God's" (Matthew 22:21). I'm sure the people in Jesus's day took a step back when they heard that and said something like "Wait a second, Jesus—these are the people you want us to respect?"

What's even more interesting is what Paul said about Caesar and his representatives in Romans 13:1–5:

> Let everyone be subject to the governing authorities, for there is no authority except that which God has established. The authorities that exist have been established by God. Consequently, whoever rebels against the authority is rebelling against what God has instituted, and those who do so will bring judgment on themselves. For rulers hold no terror for those who do right, but for those who do wrong. Do you want to be free from fear of the one in authority? Then do what is right and you will be commended. For the one in authority is God's servant for your good. But if you do wrong, be afraid, for rulers do not bear the sword for no reason. They are God's servants, agents of wrath to bring punishment on the wrongdoer. Therefore, it is necessary to submit to the authorities, not only because of possible punishment but also as a matter of conscience.

Some who have a knowledge of biblical history might be quick to speak up and say that Paul wrote those words when Christians weren't experiencing horrible persecution, because obviously he would have changed his tune if he were experiencing imperial persecution. Believe it or not, I've heard that kind of reasoning before. This argument doesn't work. To understand why, we need to look at what Peter said about politics and those in authority in his first letter. But to grasp the full context of Peter's views of political authority, we need to look at the man who had ultimate authority during the writing of this letter.

That man was Nero.

Nero's aristocratic father died when he was young, and his mother, Agrippina, wanted power. She married the Roman emperor Claudius, and thus Nero became the stepson of, and next in line to follow, the most powerful man in the world. Agrippina didn't want to wait too long, so she poisoned Claudius's dinner one evening. He died later that night, and Nero became emperor.

How do you think Nero acted as an emperor? He probably acted the way any teenager would if he had been abused, had been spoiled by his mother, and had psychopathic tendencies. This young teenager was now the most powerful person in the world and a horrible emperor. Maybe we should use the word *wicked* instead. Nero was a wicked emperor. In fact, he gave new meaning to the word.

Far from being the disciplined musician and artist he desired to be, Nero was unstable and unpredictable. He threw wild parties and orgies in his palace. He fell in love with a slave boy, surgically altered him to be like a woman, married him, and paraded him down the streets of Rome. Nero started gangs and regularly beat up people on city streets. He killed people or had them killed, including his younger stepbrother; his mentor, Seneca; wealthy individuals; and senators. After having an affair with his mom, he had her killed as well. To top off the list, he kicked his pregnant wife in the stomach, which killed her and his unborn baby.

He loved the power of being emperor, hated politicians, and wanted to be an artist. One of his dreams was to recreate Rome and make it beautiful. He was frustrated because he couldn't get much more money from the empire's already high taxes. As luck would have it, a large section of

Rome burned down. The idea surfaced that Nero or his associates started the fire to make room for his new Rome. Instead of taking responsibility, however, Nero chose to blame a certain group of people: Christians.

Because people were angry about the fire and loss of life, they went along with Nero's idea that Christians burned Rome. As a result, the first government-sanctioned persecution of Christians began. They were thrown to wild animals, brutally killed, burned like torches to light Nero's gardens, and more. Under the persecution, there was no distinction— men, women, and children were slaughtered. As a matter of fact, this very persecution would eventually claim the lives of the apostles Paul and Peter.

Depending on when scholars date the writing of 1 Peter, the letter was written either during this persecution or not too long before it. Even if Peter wrote the letter before the persecution, Nero was still a wicked, psychopathic emperor by then. In this society, Christians reached out to Peter and asked how they should respond to the hostility they were facing. Imagine how they felt watching their loved ones be tortured and killed.

Yet, while a wicked pagan emperor was leading the most powerful empire in the world, Peter implored the Christians of his day, "Show proper respect to everyone, love the family of believers, fear God, *honor the emperor*" (2:17).

Whoa . . . seriously?

How could Peter write this statement when he knew the evil and corrupt things Nero did? Did Peter really mean what he wrote there? Well, let's back up and include a few verses before verse 17, and maybe we'll see what he meant:

> *Submit yourselves* for the Lord's sake to *every* human authority: *whether to the emperor,* as the supreme authority, or to governors, who are sent by him to punish those who do wrong and to

commend those who do right. For it is God's will that by doing good you should silence the ignorant talk of foolish people. Live as free people, but do not use your freedom as a cover-up for evil; live as God's slaves. Show proper respect to everyone, love the family of believers, fear God, *honor the emperor.* (verses 13–17)

Honor.

Honor the emperor.

Honor the emperor—Nero.

Honor the emperor who is responsible for the death of your loved ones and stands against every moral aspect of your faith.

Honor the emperor.

WHY RESPECT FOR AUTHORITY IS NOT OUT OF DATE

How do we "honor the emperor" today? Where do we find the strength to respect and honor leaders we might not agree with or like? Is it even possible to follow Peter's command today?

In my opinion, it's not only *possible* but also *necessary* to "honor the emperor" today. In fact, it may be more important than ever!

Christians are in a position now to make a powerful difference in the world by showing respect to those in authority.

Now, I know this idea appears out of step with our society as it exists today. Our politics have become incredibly polarized, with the left becoming more "leftish" and the right becoming more "rightish" all the time (yes, I just invented two new words). Unfortunately, there are those in journalism and media outlets who don't seem to be helping; objective news reporting is becoming more difficult to find (if it ever truly existed before). Talk shows have become anything but "talk" shows, devoid of meaningful dialogue. Private conversations often aren't much better. Some blogs and podcasts are nothing more than venting sessions.

But because all this is true, Christians are in a position now to make a powerful difference in the world by showing respect to those in authority. We don't have to silence needed constructive criticism or mute our bold communication of the truth, but at the same time, we can show what it is like to honor God by honoring those he has allowed to temporarily occupy positions of public influence. This is a witness in itself for how to make society better in an orderly, peaceful, and loving way. It's another way of fulfilling the last part of the God of Tomorrow principle: Since tomorrow belongs to God, we can *graciously offer hope to people today.*

With the points I'm about to make, I hope I can convince you that this is true.

We Can Stand Up for What's Right—But in the Right Way

It was only a few days after the 2016 presidential election, and Donald Trump had been elected president of the United States. Multiple protests broke out around the country. Protesters even blocked freeways. I remember one such freeway. Why? Because I was on it!

I had just finished visiting a friend in a hospital near downtown Los Angeles. I hadn't planned on leaving yet, until I looked out the hospital window and saw a large crowd walking in the middle of the street below me. Immediately, I knew I had to get out of the area as soon as possible. I didn't want to be stuck there. The day before, I had heard nightmare stories from people who had been held up on the freeway for hours, and I was determined not to have the same experience.

As quickly as I could, I said goodbye to my friend, grabbed my stuff, and headed toward the parking garage. By the time I got out on the streets in my car, the backup had already begun. I made a big mistake and listened to the directions from the Maps app on my phone. Soon I was on the freeway . . . and stuck there for about three hours.

Now, it wasn't as bad as you might think. I got a lot of work done, returned phone calls, and even watched a TV show from Netflix. My mood changed, however, when I had to use the bathroom. I tried to ignore it, but the pressure kept building minute after minute, and I sat there stressed out about it. Eventually, the protesters moved out of the way and we were able to go forward. I've never pulled off the freeway and found a bathroom so quickly in all my life.

While that is a funny story, unfortunately the protests ended up causing severe difficulty for people who needed to get to important appointments or go to the hospital. Some protestors were even hit by cars that refused to stop on the freeway. Maybe you remember all that mayhem. I remember thinking, *Is this how we handle our disapproval and disagreement with our leaders?*

If Peter saw Christians behaving this way, he would have immediately tried to stop it. He'd probably agree that the more venomous and destructive we get, the less our voices are heard and the more the real issue is overshadowed by our lack of self-control. When it comes to voicing our opinions, we are in desperate need of self-control. We can stand for justice, healthy morals, and strong ethics without alienating others or causing them frustration. For example, standing in a freeway isn't the best way to garner the attention we want. Venting in one social media post after another won't sway people. They'll just skip over our posts and eventually unfollow us, unfriend us, or whatever "un-" word you want to use. If we're directing every conversation to a platform for our political opinions, people will stop having conversations with us. Hey, if I did that

I'd stop having conversations with myself! Let's stand up for the right things in the right way.

We Can Respect the Positions That Leaders Hold Even If We Don't Think Highly of the Leaders Themselves

No matter how many times I read the words Peter wrote—"honor the emperor"—I feel convicted. Why? Because I haven't done a good job of honoring presidents, governors, senators, representatives, judges, mayors, and other officials. When I contemplate the way Peter instructed Christians to live under the first Roman persecution, I wonder, *Who am I to unintentionally mock the holy lives of the martyrs by crying "Persecution!" during a time when God has allowed us to still hold on to religious freedom?* If God were to compare my attitude with the attitude of those who were fed to animals and burned like torches, would he approve?

Just in case you didn't know, the answer is a resounding *no*.

When the writers of the New Testament talked about politics, they mainly pointed out *our* responsibility, how *we* treat people in authority, and so on—no matter what. I don't think Jesus, Paul, or any other leader in the Bible would say that submission is weak or that we should deny the fundamentals of our faith. Here's what they do want us to understand: God takes it personally when we disrespect leaders.

In our society today, we don't like to dialogue about our role and responsibility to leadership; we want the tables turned. We want to talk about how our leaders are not living up to our standards. Now, in a republic, we have every right to do so and should do so. But before we ever look at anyone else, we should double-check our posture and how we are responding to our leaders. We can show respect to them because of the offices they hold, even if we don't care for them (and that may be putting it very lightly) as persons or politicians. Use caution in what you say and write. Respect the office even if you don't like the individual occupying it.

Honoring Leaders, Even Bad Ones, Is Part of Our Worship of God

My respect for those in authority doesn't have its foundation in the individuals who are leading. Instead, my respect for leaders originates from my trust in God. I choose to submit to authority because I trust God. I know he has a plan, and because he is sovereign, perhaps he's seen some things further down the corridor of time that I am not privy to yet.

Why does our attitude toward those in authority matter so much to God? Here's my opinion (and it's just that—my opinion): God says, "Trust me to handle it, and your struggles with them today won't be part of tomorrow."

What if God wants to grow my trust in him when I'm in submission to leaders I disagree with? What if he wants to strengthen my kindness by putting me in situations where I have every chance to run down a leader but refuse? What if God wants me to work harder to see the potential in any person? What if he desires that I have a stronger prayer life, so he allows me to have a frustrated heart that leads me to him? Anytime we go to God, rely on him, and choose to obey and follow him, that's worship.

My respect for my leaders, even the poor ones, is one of the ways I'm able to worship God. It's like what the prophet Daniel wrote:

> Praise be to the name of God for ever and ever;
>> wisdom and power are his.
> He changes times and seasons;
>> he deposes kings and raises up others.
> He gives wisdom to the wise
>> and knowledge to the discerning.
> He reveals deep and hidden things;
>> he knows what lies in darkness,
>> and light dwells with him. (2:20–22)

Bad Leadership Reminds Us to Hope in God's Tomorrow

The power to have courage in the face of any brutal leader is found in the sovereignty of God. As we discussed earlier, the power of God that has fashioned tomorrow will sustain us today. Peter pointed us to the hope of tomorrow with the first few verses of his book:

> Praise be to the God and Father of our Lord Jesus Christ! In his great mercy he has given us new birth into a living hope through the resurrection of Jesus Christ from the dead, and into an inheritance that can never perish, spoil or fade. This inheritance is kept in heaven for you, who through faith are shielded by God's power until the coming of the salvation that is ready to be revealed in the last time. . . . You believe in him and are filled with an inexpressible and glorious joy, for you are receiving the end result of your faith, the salvation of your souls. (1 Peter 1:3–5, 8–9)

As I've mentioned a few times before, we forget that Jesus and the apostles said their words when Israel was under an oppressive, occupying, pagan, religion-restricting, brutal, murderous Roman Empire being led by a series of dictators who thought they were divine. Yet because Jesus and leaders such as Paul and Peter believed in God's control of tomorrow, they could have faith that was bigger than the Roman Empire.

Whatever leaders do while they have authority, God brings good out of the good and even good out of the bad.

God alone is sovereign. Regardless of whether leaders do good things or bad things, God has an unfolding plan. He's the one responsible to raise up leaders and remove leaders. Whatever leaders do while they have authority, God brings good out of the good and even good out of the bad. Since he is sovereign and has raised up leaders, it is up to him to deal with them. When we disrespect and dishonor leaders, we're taking a liberty that never belonged to us.

LOOK TO THE COMING KINGDOM

I've already mentioned the prophet Daniel more than once. He was one of the Israelites held captive in Babylon, yet he gained favor among the kings he served under. In the early days of Daniel's service to Babylon, King Nebuchadnezzar had a dream that disturbed him. His wisest counselors couldn't unlock the mystery of it. Daniel, however, was able to give the king the answer. Daniel 2:31–35 says,

> Your Majesty looked, and there before you stood a large statue—an enormous, dazzling statue, awesome in appearance. The head of the statue was made of pure gold, its chest and arms of silver, its belly and thighs of bronze, its legs of iron, its feet partly of iron and partly of baked clay. While you were watching, a rock was cut out, but not by human hands. It struck the statue on its feet of iron and clay and smashed them. Then the iron, the clay, the bronze, the silver and the gold were all broken to pieces and became like chaff on a threshing floor in the summer. The wind swept them away without leaving a trace. But the rock that struck the statue became a huge mountain and filled the whole earth.

When one reads about the dream of Nebuchadnezzar, it almost seems like a Tim Burton movie. Imagine reading this for the first time; it definitely seems wacky! Yet through this dream, God gave the king a glimpse of what tomorrow would look like. Biblical scholar Stephen R. Miller provides an excellent account:

> Daniel . . . interpreted the first kingdom to be the ancient Babylonian Empire represented by its king, Nebuchadnezzar. For sixty-six years (605–539 B.C.) the Neo-Babylonian Empire ruled the Near East.
>
> Daniel disclosed that another "kingdom" would rise after the Babylonian Empire. History is plain that the next great power to appear on the world scene was the Medo-Persian Empire led by the dynamic Cyrus the Great. This empire is symbolized by the silver chest and arms of the great statue, the two arms conceivably representing the two parts or divisions of the empire. Medo-Persian dominance continued for approximately 208 years (539–331 B.C.).[1]

The transition of power, as represented by the statue, continued:

> The empire that followed Medo-Persia was Greece. In 332 B.C. the armies of the great conqueror Alexander the Great marched against the Medo-Persian Empire and defeated it in a series of decisive battles. The Greek Empire dominated for approximately 185 years (331–146 B.C.).[2]

The fourth kingdom was the Roman Empire.

> [It] dominated the world from the defeat of Carthage in 146 B.C. to the division of the East and West empires in A.D. 395, approximately five hundred years. The last Roman emperor ruled in the West until A.D. 476, and the Eastern division of the empire continued until A.D. 1453.[3]

These are some incredibly strong kingdoms. But what about what verse 34 says: "A rock was cut out, but not by human hands"? What is that rock?

Daniel explained the meaning of the rock in verses 44–45:

> In the time of those kings, the God of heaven will set up a king-
> dom that will never be destroyed, nor will it be left to another
> people. It will crush all those kingdoms and bring them to an
> end, but it will itself endure forever. This is the meaning of the
> vision of the rock cut out of a mountain, but not by human
> hands—a rock that broke the iron, the bronze, the clay, the silver
> and the gold to pieces.
>
> The great God has shown the king what will take place in
> the future. The dream is true and its interpretation is trustworthy.

No pun intended, but one line blows me away: "The wind swept them away without leaving a trace" (verse 35). It was as if the nations never existed. If you go to the right places, you can see the ruins of ancient Egypt, Roman cities, and other historical buildings. Even though the decay of time has swept over these buildings, you can still get a glimpse of how magnificent they were. Yet this kingdom has come, outlasted every other kingdom, and will fill the whole earth. The kingdoms of the earth share an ultimate purpose: to set the scene for the most powerful kingdom to fill the earth.

This world has seen its share of powerful nations, empires, and dynasties:
- the Egyptians under various pharaonic dynasties
- the Babylonians
- Alexander the Great's empire
- the Roman Empire

- the Mongol Empire
- the Tang Dynasty
- the Inca Empire
- the Ottoman Empire
- the United States

None of these compare to the power of the kingdom that God will establish.

The end of verse 35 paints a picture of what tomorrow will look like: "The rock that struck the statue became a huge mountain and filled the whole earth." The time is coming when the kingdom will fill the whole world, but the King is already reigning.

God is on his throne. He won't relinquish it. He's not pacing back and forth with anxiety, wondering how things will turn out.

Here's the good news, and I hope it resonates with you:

- If the church survived Nero, it'll survive any president.
- If the church outlasted Idi Amin and Muammar Gaddafi, it'll thrive in a republic.
- If the church made it past Hitler and Stalin, it'll grow past any evil.
- If the church outlived Mao Zedong, it will continue to outlive any leader.
- If the church survived Roosevelt, Truman, Eisenhower, Kennedy, Johnson, Nixon, Ford, Carter, Reagan, Bush, Clinton, Bush, Obama, Trump, and _____, then it will always be fine. The church will continually exist because it's sustained and relies on the power of God. Jesus promised in Matthew 16:18 that not even the gates of hell will overcome the church.

We need to be respectful of our leaders, whoever they are, because of the authority granted to them temporarily by God. That doesn't mean we must like them or like what they are doing to our society. But we can take comfort in the bigger picture that Christianity has outlasted and will outlast any one person who leads a political party, city, state, country, gang, or empire. There's great freedom in knowing that our faith doesn't rely on the politics of any one person or nation. Our faith rests securely in the rule of God on earth today and his promise for a better tomorrow.

REFLECTION AND DISCUSSION QUESTIONS

1. Read Matthew 22:21 and Romans 13:1–5. What did Jesus and Paul say about respecting our authorities?

2. After learning more about Nero, how do you feel when you read 1 Peter 2:17? Do you agree or disagree with what Peter was imploring?

3. How can we stand up for justice, hurting people, and a broken society while not being disrespectful to our leaders? What's the difference between voicing our opinions and maligning authority? How have you seen this in society?

4. According to Daniel 2:21–22, how does God exercise his complete authority over those with temporary authority?

5. How is treating our leaders with respect a way of worshipping God? Have you done this well recently? Why or why not? What can you do to either start or continue to treat your leaders with respect?

IN AN
EVER-CHANGING,
DIVERSE SOCIETY,
OUR GOAL ISN'T
TO MAKE PEOPLE
MORE LIKE US BUT
TO INTRODUCE
THEM TO JESUS
THROUGH THE
GOSPEL.

10

No More Christian Bullies

"She's just not where she needs to be." That's how the person who had been meeting with my mom to study the Bible started the conversation with me.

A few weeks prior to this phone call, my family and I had transitioned from Dallas to Southern California. Right before we left, my mom and dad both gave their lives to the Lord. It completely floored me because each told me about his or her decision within the same week and they hadn't even talked to each other about it. Ironic, huh? That's the way God works: in mystery and irony.

Since we had left, more than one person had seen it as their job to teach my mom what it means to be a Christian. They had no idea my mom and I had regular conversations about faith and God. Part of me thinks that even if they had known, it wouldn't have mattered. They might still have wanted to push their views on her.

New Christians learn early on about the fundamentals of the faith (God, the Trinity, Jesus, salvation, and so on). Stay a Christian long enough, and you'll be tempted to begin to add to the list of fundamentals you and others *have* to keep. You could begin to think of others' political views, friendships, possessions, and other things as additions to your fundamental list. Such thinking is a clear pathway to Christian bullying.

I understand that the people who were meeting with my mom did so because they honestly wanted to help her understand Scripture. I had no issue with that. The problem for me was that these people seemed to be more interested in my mom's understanding *their view* of Scripture. This bothered me.

"Caleb, I know you say she's saved," one woman told me, "but have you heard her thoughts on issues like hell?"

"Yes, I have," I replied. "My mom has lived her whole life away from God. It will take time for her to study and learn more about what the Bible says and why she believes what she believes."

My answer didn't satisfy the person on the other end of the line. "She should believe this now. We're meeting with her to make sure she believes the correct things about the Bible."

I paused. Sometimes you must pause and take a moment so you don't say the wrong thing. When my moment had passed, I began to speak my mind. "If that's what you're doing, you should probably make plans not to meet with her anymore. When you say you want her to know the 'correct things about the Bible,' that worries me, because I don't even agree with you on most of what you believe." (If I had a longer book, I could outline in detail the theological differences I had with the person I was talking to, but we don't have that kind of time.)

Ignoring my words, the individual retorted, "We've got this new curriculum that was just released, and we're going to introduce it to her." The Bible study material they were going to share with her was written from a very conservative theological and political standpoint. I knew of the study and agreed with most of what was in it. However, the people wanting to study with my mom were so concerned about her having the same beliefs as they did that they had forgotten who they were dealing with.

My mom was one of the most liberal Democrats I knew. She despised most Republicans, still disdained most Christians (though she believed in Jesus), couldn't stand the phrase *family values,* and was very particular about what church or Bible study she would attend after I left Dallas. I knew this about my mom, but the people talking to her didn't. Unfortunately, they hadn't taken the time to get to know her as a person. They were more worried about how quickly they could help her understand theology as they understood it. When they did run into my mom's political views and lingering bitterness against conservative Christians, they took it as a sign of immaturity. I took it as a sign of how she had lived and believed most of her life; it was something she would have to wrestle through to forgive. I knew there were many elements about her that would never meet their expectations.

"Why don't you get to know her?" I asked. My question wasn't rocket science. One didn't need a Harvard law degree to figure out the solution. Missionaries would say the solution is "contextualization" (getting to know the culture they are ministering to). Other people, such as you and me, would call it "common sense" or "care" or even "empathy."

This person eventually stopped meeting with my mom. I was glad. It meant so much to me that people were willing to meet with her regularly. It meant so little to me that some were after clones rather than companions. They were seeking to convince her of their particular worldviews rather than do the hard work of listening to and understanding her.

This person was a legalist. Now, one aspect of legalism is proudly obeying the rules and thinking we are earning God's approval by doing it. But there's another ugly, and more public, face of legalism: trying to force one's view of biblical morality on people who aren't ready for it. This was definitely the type of legalism being inflicted on my mom.

This second type of legalism is tempting to all of us, but it's the opposite of the kind of relationship investment we should be engaging in. Honestly, I consider it bullying. It's nothing like how Jesus dealt with people.

In an ever-changing, diverse society, our goal isn't to make people more like us but to introduce them to Jesus through the gospel. Engagement with society means introducing others to the one who loves them and can change them from the inside. Tomorrow belongs to God, so we can graciously offer hope to people today. Let him prepare people for the future he has for them.

If you are a legalistic person who is bullying others, then, in the famous words of Bob Newhart, *stop it!*[1] You are better than how you're acting and you have a better God than how you're behaving. So . . . *stop it!*

> **In an ever-changing, diverse society, our goal isn't to make people more like us but to introduce them to Jesus through the gospel.**

You might say you're not the kind of person who treats others as projects instead of people, trying to force them to conform to your view of what's right and true. And you may be right—I hope so! I certainly believe that legalistic tendencies can be unlearned. But I think we should all stop every once in a while and ask ourselves if we've been getting into bad habits with how we treat those who don't follow Jesus and those who are new followers of Jesus. We need to continually renew our commitment to *graciously* hold out hope to others.

Even if you're not a legalist, you probably know one. So read on, because now we're going to find out how Jesus dealt with someone like that.

AN EVENING MEETING THAT *NEVER* HAPPENED

It was nighttime—probably late at night—when the meeting was set. Two religious leaders were about to meet and discuss theology. Why was the meeting set for the dark of night? Because one of the leaders didn't want to get caught. This sneaky religious leader was a man named Nicodemus. He was a Pharisee and a member of the Sanhedrin, which was the religious leadership council. Nicodemus and his fellow Pharisees had an understanding of the entire Hebrew Scriptures unlike anything we see today. He came to Jesus, the talked-about new rabbi in town, ready to have a theological dialogue.

Each arrived at the meeting, and as it appears from John 3:2, Nicodemus was the first one to speak: "Rabbi, we know that you are a teacher who has come from God. For no one could perform the signs you are doing if God were not with him." Perhaps he started off the conversation with Jesus like this because he really did believe that Jesus came from God. Or maybe Nicodemus was hoping to bring Jesus's presumed defenses down with a compliment. I don't know.

In any case, he learned quickly that Jesus wasn't after compliments or compromise that evening—he was about to teach Nicodemus a thing or two about God. Jesus replied, "Very truly I tell you, no one can see the kingdom of God unless they are born again" (verse 3).

Nicodemus responded probably much like you and I would if we were him: "How can someone be born when they are old? . . . Surely they cannot enter a second time into their mother's womb to be born!" (verse 4).

Can you blame Nicodemus? I have a pretty thick skull, and it takes a while for me to understand some things. It's easy for Christians to read this story and think, *Knucklehead Nicodemus,* because we know the end of the story and the hope of tomorrow. But Nicodemus was without the New Testament, so he was learning for the first time.

Jesus wasn't concerned with winning an argument with a legalistic Pharisee. He really desired for Nicodemus to understand the truth. So he continued, "Very truly I tell you, no one can enter the kingdom of God unless they are born of water and the Spirit. Flesh gives birth to flesh, but the Spirit gives birth to spirit. You should not be surprised at my saying, 'You must be born again.' The wind blows wherever it pleases. You hear its sound, but you cannot tell where it comes from or where it is going. So it is with everyone born of the Spirit" (verses 5–8).

Nicodemus was floored by Jesus's logic and theology, so he engaged Jesus even more. "How can this be?" (verse 9).

I have to say that I like Nicodemus at this point. Elsewhere in the Gospels, we learn that Jesus knew that in the hearts of some men, there was a desire to kill him. But this is never said about Nicodemus. He's like those people we engage who aren't out to get us but truly are interested in God.

One of the reasons I love this dialogue is because of the example Jesus set under these circumstances. He could have made Nicodemus feel horrible, but instead he chided him just a little bit:

> "You are Israel's teacher," said Jesus, "and do you not understand these things? Very truly I tell you, we speak of what we know, and we testify to what we have seen, but still you people do not accept our testimony. I have spoken to you of earthly things and you do not believe; how then will you believe if I speak of heavenly things? No one has ever gone into heaven except the one who came from heaven—the Son of Man. Just as Moses lifted up the snake in the wilderness, so the Son of Man must be lifted up, that everyone who believes may have eternal life in him." (verses 10–15)

So let's review. Jesus reminded Nicodemus,
- I've seen things you have not.
- What you see here is a shadow of what lies in heaven.
- I have a greater purpose than what you know.

- I will be "lifted up" so that redemption and eternal life will arrive for people.
- You don't understand it, but you have a witness of it right before you.

Jesus has seen things we haven't. He has seen what tomorrow will hold; we haven't. So he could tell Nicodemus, in effect, "God has a grander plan for tomorrow than what you might think. It's much bigger than any religious custom. God's plan for tomorrow is greater than your traditions."

One can imagine that Nicodemus's eyes were fixed on Jesus, unaware of the truth bomb that was about to hit him. Jesus moved on with one of the most famous verses around. Even if you don't know the Bible well or at all, I'm sure you've heard of this famous verse: "God so loved the world that he gave his one and only Son, that whoever believes in him shall not perish but have eternal life" (verse 16).

Another review is in order. Jesus was saying,

- God has a plan for tomorrow.
- I will accomplish it.
- The plan is open to the whole world, not just Israel.
- God's plan is to save the world.
- He will save the world through me, his Son.
- Whoever believes in the Son will join God in tomorrow.

Nicodemus was speechless, body frozen, and unsure of what to even ask next. If what Jesus said was true, the oral traditions and human-imposed applications of his brand of Judaism were wrong. Not only that, but his particular way of Judaism was alienating those in the Gentile world and many in the Jewish world.

Nicodemus—once certain that the legalistic, micromanaging, rule-keeping Pharisee version of Judaism was the way to follow—began to understand the possible flaws of his beliefs.

SPIRITUAL PRIDE MANAGEMENT

None of us sets out to be a legalist, hypocrite, or "bully for Jesus." It's easy to slip into this mode unknowingly. Here's how it often works: We admit our need for God, submit to Christ, commit to living for him, start telling our friends about Jesus and inviting them to church, realize that the Bible has a lot of depth and develop a hunger to learn about it, start to focus too much on how we feel and what theology we know . . . and one day realize we don't feel compassion for those who don't understand our faith. We feel frustration.

It happens to every one of us—our insecurities use our relationship with God, given by God, to benefit ourselves or make ourselves feel good. It almost seems as though our sinful nature is jumping at the chance to create an obstacle between us and others who need to hear the message of Jesus. Subtly, our mind-set becomes *What can God do for me today?* or *What can I get from God?*

Let's face it: legalists can be hard to love. And it's difficult when you and I realize we have the capacity to be legalistic too. Hopefully you've seen the danger that comes from spiritual bullying. When we feel the spiritual bully in all of us get stronger, we need to counter with some spiritual pride management. For our purposes, let's take notice of a few things Jesus did with Nicodemus and other people he encountered.

Surrender the Need to Evaluate Others

During a trip to Chicago, I was really looking forward to my coffee time with Derrick and Karen, some old friends of mine who had moved there. After losing contact with them for a while, I had finally reconnected with them and was eager to hear about what was going on in their lives.

In the middle of the conversation, I asked how church was going for them.

Following a brief silence, Derrick said, "I'm not really going to church right now. I don't feel safe."

Neither Derrick nor Karen were attending the church where they had been members for many years. Karen was visiting churches and had found one she thought she might go to regularly. She replied with a comment that made me pause: "I couldn't worship in our former church because there were many people I had unreconciled differences with. We just seemed to go through the motions on Sunday."

Wow!

She went on to say that they didn't fit the mold of their old church and were looked down on for even thinking of visiting another church. She said that she felt *evaluated*.

Later that evening, the conversation I had with them wouldn't leave me. I began to think of a lot of churches I knew and how in some of the unhealthier ones, people attended, served, and lifted hands together, all while allowing grudges and unexpressed feelings to govern their hearts. Perhaps you've seen this type of behavior from religious people in society before. These people come with orthodox doctrine and an unparalleled grasp of Scripture, but they lack the love and graciousness that compel people to see God's heart. While I love these people very much, they've retreated into a mind-set of isolation. When Christians reach the point of isolating themselves as a means of dealing with the direction of society, they become legalistic. They operate by "the rules." Unfortunately, this legalistic and isolationist mind-set won't save them, and it will create a blockade to those who need to follow Jesus.

To be fair, it's not just traditionalist religious people who can be legalistic and evaluate others. It can also be people who are champions of tolerance or stringent social justice warriors. Such people have their own list of dos and don'ts that you shouldn't violate unless you want to be cast to the side.

In my years of ministering in the Southern California area, I've met my share of celebrities who attend church. You might even be surprised at which movie stars, pop stars, and sports stars are Christian. Here's the thing, though: many don't talk about it publicly, nor do they want anyone to know they lean slightly toward the right when it comes to politics. Why? They've told me it's a well-known fact that if you are a strong Christian or even hint at Republican views, it's easy to be tossed to the side of Hollywood. Another way to say it: their career would be in jeopardy. It seems Christian legalists aren't the only ones out there who are good at using a list to evaluate people.

First-century Pharisees were spectacular at evaluating others to cover up their own flaws. For more information, check out how Jesus described these hypocrites in Matthew chapters 6 and 23. At some point in their spiritual walk, almost all Christians will be tempted to evaluate others. Their pride will lure them to use their faith to create bubbles that separate them from the society God loves. But if we allow our Christian culture to become legalistic so we'll be "safe" from the world, we compromise our engagement of those far from God. We become indifferent toward society. It's easy to fall into this trap.

If you remember where you've come from, it will be hard to be prideful about who you are.

The more I read this account, the more I'm struck with how Jesus interacted with Nicodemus. Unlike Pharisees such as Nicodemus, Jesus didn't evaluate. He listened to this religious leader. Before Jesus let any words fly from his mouth, he made sure to hear. Nicodemus may have arrived with a preparation to argue. Jesus didn't. He wanted to make a difference in this religious zealot's life. Those who are legalistic love to argue. Why argue with them? Arguing with people who love to argue assures that you're playing their game.

Remember who you are. Yes, you are a saved individual, but you are a saved individual who is still sinful at your core. While you may have made great strides forward in life because of God's help, neither you nor anyone else has ever reached perfection. If you remember where you've come from, it will be hard to be prideful about who you are.

Watch How You Talk About Others

A friend of mine, Ben Cachiaras, recently posted on Twitter, "I think it's wrong to be rude, even in the name of morality, even if there's a lot on the line and I am convinced I am right." Amen, Ben! Amen—times one hundred. Just because you passionately disagree with someone doesn't mean you discard that person with your words. It's fascinating to me that in a day of supposed tolerance, those same people believe that one offense deserves another.

In the next chapter we'll be looking much more at how we use words to represent our Lord in a diverse and changing society. But here I just want to point out that our words matter. Part of how people evaluate the way they feel about a person, organization, or event is by examining their experience. If their experience with people isn't good, don't expect them to come rushing back another time.

Imagine that some of us went to a new restaurant. We'd heard good things about it, so naturally it seemed right to try it out. After paying our bill and walking outside, we started talking about the night. The food was good enough to the point where we wouldn't mind coming back to eat. However, we probably won't be coming back. Why? Because the servers were so rude. Maybe it would have been excusable if it were just one, but three servers we interacted with were rude. They looked impatiently at their watches while we were ordering, intentionally ignored our attempts to get their attention, and argued with us when we pointed out that our meals were wrong. Basically, the servers were indifferent toward us, and in the absence of an apology, we were left to assume they didn't care about us. I'm not sure about you, but I probably wouldn't go back, nor would I recommend the restaurant to others.

While Nicodemus may have felt many things about this meeting, we know he had no grounds to feel that Jesus was harsh with him. Jesus wanted his heart softened.

Be You and Only You

Besides the presence of God, do you know what the most powerful aspect of you is? You. Exactly you. Your personality. Your perspective. Your story. And so you—the real you—is what you need to show others. Be yourself. Don't be afraid to share your victories as well as your faults.

> **There is nothing, nothing, nothing more repelling to society than Christians being inauthentic about who they are.**

I'm not saying God doesn't need to work on us. Rather, I'm saying too many of us go about life with a facade that hides who we really are. How many of us

- put on a fake smile and act as though we love when we don't?
- know worship songs by heart but wound others during the week with words?
- seek to impress with Bible knowledge but continually manipulate at work?

- nod to agree with the sermon but mistreat our loved ones?
- are passionate about church polity but show no concern for hurting people?

I appreciate what best-selling author David Kinnaman said about the refusal to be ourselves:

What are Christians known for? Outsiders think our moralizing, our condemnations, and our attempts to draw boundaries around everything. Even if these standards are accurate and biblical, they seem to be all we have to offer. And our lives are a poor advertisement for the standards. We have set the game board to register lifestyle points; then we are surprised to be trapped by our mistakes. The truth is we have invited the hypocrite image.[2]

Listen to me on this: there is nothing, nothing, nothing more repelling to society than Christians being inauthentic about who they are. I can assure you that if you don't want to effectively share the hope of Jesus with the younger generations of your society, all you have to do is be fake, be invulnerable, be a hypocrite, and put up walls.

Jesus was exactly who he was in this conversation with Nicodemus. Your authenticity and transparency about where you are with God will be more attractive to people than you think. And even if they don't admit it, your vulnerability will be compelling to the really strong legalists!

GRACE AND GLORY

As followers of Jesus, we're called to lead people to love God and love people. If John 3:16 has taught us anything, it's that grace is for everyone. It's because of grace that we can offer hope to people today! Believing that grace excludes others isn't just bad theology; it creates negative attitudes toward the very people in our society whom you and I are called to pursue by sharing God's hope for tomorrow.

I can't help but wonder if you and I have had bullying attitudes toward others. Don't misunderstand me—I'm not saying this is something we have intended to do, but I'm willing to bet that, however unintentionally, we've done it. As you find yourself in conflict with someone, do you start telling your side of the story to others and exaggerating the circumstances? Do these people know both sides of the story, or have they just merely accepted your label of the person or situation? Do you ever find yourself secretly writing off people when you discover they admire a certain movie star, watch a particular news channel, or listen to a certain preacher? Are there times you've become combative with people when they disagree with you? What needs to happen in your heart to make such spiritual pride or indifference vanish for good?

When we as Christians allow spiritual pride to foster indifference toward others, it compromises the message of God's hope for tomorrow that we're called to share with people. It reinforces the belief that some in our society hold—that God and his promises for tomorrow are irrelevant. It is a surefire way to keep broken and hurting people away from our doors. Authenticity about who we are is the way we model humanity's ultimate need for grace.

Maybe Derrick is right. Perhaps most churches aren't safe. Maybe churches try as much as they can to be safe, but are we safe when we're surrounded by other broken people like us? Maybe the goal isn't to be safe—it might be that the goal is to be *intentional* in pointing people to tomorrow, just as Jesus was.

Before you conclude that I'm just another person beating up on Christians, let me reassure you that I don't think all believers are as I've described. Here's the point: the mission to let society know that the God of Tomorrow gave his Son for them is too costly for *any* Christian to be legalistic. I agree with Charles Spurgeon: "The salvation of God is for those who do not deserve it and have no preparation for it."[3] God gets the most glory when people follow his Son. God gets the glory when those who were far from him follow his Son, learn about God, and pursue others who are far away from God. As followers who are to continue the ministry of Jesus's first coming, maybe we need to keep John 3:17 in mind: "God did not send his Son into the world to condemn the world, but to save the world through him."

Far from condemnation, we need grace. To fight our bullying tendencies, we need to put our faith *in motion*. Perhaps Jesus followers should ask questions such as, "How can I partner with my faith community to invite my friends and family to church?" Perhaps we can learn a more loving and effective way of sharing Jesus with others. If that's what you want, keep reading.

REFLECTION AND DISCUSSION QUESTIONS

1. Have you ever been or seen a Christian bully in action? What happened and how did the person being bullied seem to feel? Did it draw her to God or push her further from God?

2. Read John 3:1–21. Jesus told Nicodemus what he needed to know, not exactly what he wanted to know. According to the passage, what did Nicodemus need to know?

3. As your typical day progresses, which do you ask yourself more: "What can God do for me today?" or "What can I do for God?" What's the difference between the two questions?

4. How does pride foster indifference? Have you ever seen this in your life?

5. Why is authenticity an antidote for pride? What makes authenticity so powerful?

WHEN PEOPLE LOOK AT YOUR LIFE, IT SHOULD BE SO EASY FOR THEM TO SEE JESUS IN HOW YOU TREAT THEM, LOVE THEM, AND SHARE TRUTH WITH THEM.

11

Bullhorns Aren't Loud Enough

If you've ever been to Third Street Promenade in Santa Monica, you know it's quite the experience. There are some amazing restaurants and eccentric clothing stores in that little area, the beach is nearby, there's a boardwalk pier with a mini amusement park on it, and you can even hop on Pacific Coast Highway and be in Malibu in a matter of minutes (if traffic allows you).

What fascinates me the most about Third Street, though, are the people. If you think there is a stereotype of a person who lives in Southern California, then you've never been to Southern California. There is every type of person in this area—*every* type.

When I go down to the promenade, my favorite thing to do is to go mullet hunting. For some reason, it seems as though many people in Santa Monica have mullets. I mean, who doesn't love a good mullet? How could you not love a business-in-the-front, party-in-the-back haircut? Good stuff!

When you visit Santa Monica, you'll find YouTube stars, TV personalities, and others doing interviews on the sidewalk, performing magic tricks, orchestrating pranks, playing in bands so they'll get noticed, and more. At times there might be Christians with microphones or bullhorns yelling about Jesus and sin to those walking by. Some have skits they do, and then they talk about them on the bullhorn. Others have scripts they say over and over again on the bullhorn. A few will even have dramatic props while they talk about the gospel.

I'm not sure about where you live, but in Southern California we have a lot of bullhorn preachers. I guess we need them. I even remember seeing bullhorn preachers when I went to a preseason game in which the Los Angeles Rams were playing my awesome Kansas City Chiefs.

Now, before you think I'm attacking bullhorn preachers, please understand I'm not. While I don't think theirs is the most effective way of sharing Christ in our modern-day society, I do know people who accepted Christ because of hearing a message from a bullhorn preacher. I also know there were other events that transpired in their lives that got them to the place where they were ready to hear the message, but nonetheless, the bullhorn was the icing on the top. Basically, if it helps someone trust Jesus, I'm for it!

In general, however, I believe we've gotten to a point in our society where bullhorn preaching isn't as impactful as maybe it once was. There is no bullhorn loud enough for people to pay attention to you. Most of the time, it blends in with all the other noise. There's so much clamor now that people are okay with whatever a person wants to believe as long as it doesn't hurt anyone.

A lot of the more traditional approaches to sharing Jesus with others no longer work well in our changed society, and I imagine they will only become less effective tomorrow as society continues to become more spiritually and religiously diverse. Does that mean we should give up and retreat into our own groups because "those people out there" don't care about God? Of course not. God is just as much the almighty Sovereign today and tomorrow as he ever was. We just need to find ways to share the gospel of the Savior in ways that actually get through to people and aren't counterproductive.

Forming relationships, helping those in need, paying special attention to those who don't have a place in society, avoiding the victim mentality and hypocrisy, keeping up a respectful attitude toward leaders—these are all important. But sooner or later we'll have the chance to tell people the Jesus story and how it intersects with our own story and theirs. The gospel is good *news,* after all. How are we going to share it in a mosaic society?

THE ATHENS SCHOOL OF SOCIAL ENGAGEMENT

If there was anyone who lived in a time of polarizing beliefs, differing worldviews, obscure ideas, and competing systems, it was Paul. Yet he, like Jesus, is such a tremendous example of someone who was masterful in communicating a steadfast gospel to an ever-shifting society.

We see a glimpse of Paul's approach when he shared the gospel with Epicurean and Stoic philosophers in Acts 17:16–34. I believe Paul's interactions in this passage can help us see the importance of studying society as we strive to be intentional in sharing Jesus with others.

Verse 16 says that Paul was "greatly distressed" to see Athens full of idolatry. He was angered because such a city full of idolatry was robbing God of the glory he deserved.

Notice that Luke, the author of Acts, didn't say Paul "was greatly moved to be proved right" or "greatly desired to show them how wrong they were." He was never a bully. Rather, throughout the passage, we easily notice Paul's care and concern for these scholars. Ultimately, he was burdened for these people to become followers of God, because God gets the glory when people submit their lives to him. Paul's burden drove him to share the message of Jesus with them and not battle with them, because he was filled with a desire to show them the way to God.

After Paul finished his sermon, the philosophers asked him to stay and teach more. Instead of enjoying superstar status, he left because his goal wasn't to be right in their eyes. He was hardly concerned about trading philosophical or theological ideas for fun. Paul desired for them to know the truth. His immediate departure wasn't rude; instead, I think, it was a way of showing them he had told them the truth and cared too much for them to make them think he was interested in trading ideas (or being correct).

If our goal is to use God's words as a billy club, proving to others that we're right and they're wrong, our influence will fade. Paul, like Jesus, was concerned for the salvation of others to the glory of God. We should be as well.

Here are some takeaways from Paul at the Areopagus that you can use in Santa Monica, your town, and anywhere.

Don't Be a Society Hermit—Study Your Surroundings

We can have correct theology or good ideas from a Scripture passage, yet it may not matter. We can't share effectively with a society we haven't studied or experienced. I don't care if it's a rural town in Kansas or the booming city of Tokyo—we have to study not only the general facts about a community and the state or district and country it belongs to but also the immediate context of the people we'll be sharing the gospel with.

Let me acknowledge something: nothing I just mentioned is easy!

The study of Scripture is necessary, and we shouldn't rush it. The integrity of the Bible deserves to be examined and prayed through. Like God, Scripture never changes but is infinitely deep. We are always discovering new insights and uncovering fascinating applications from the text.

Society is different, though. People's ideas, trends, hot topics, focus, politics, and so on are always shifting. A person could understand society one year and then find the next year that his understanding is already somewhat out of date. Keeping up to date with society is a difficult but necessary task. It was something Paul dedicated himself to (and he was an expert at studying culture because he started several churches in different contexts).

Knowing that the Athenians were fascinated with idols, Paul made a theological and philosophical argument: because God is immaterial and timeless, idols are not accurate representations of him (Acts 17:24–25, 29). He then scratched the surface on one of their biggest topics: life's purpose. Paul did so by discussing God's sovereignty (verses 26–27).

Some Christians hide from society. I even have pastor friends who don't study society. Every weekend they unpack the Bible to their congregation with no mention or example of how Scripture intersects with the world around their congregation. Leaders who preach this way are like cultural hermits. Most people who attend church aren't. They go to their jobs and work day in and day out in the culture—the very society some preachers fear. You and I do not have to *make* the Bible relevant, but instead we *reveal* how the Bible is relevant to the everyday person in society. This looks different depending on the context. Each church is set in a different society. Whether a small farming community, a church plant in New York, a ministry in India, a busy corporation in Silicon Valley, or wherever the Lord has placed us, our society has to be studied and understood.

You and I do not have to *make* the Bible relevant, but instead we *reveal* how the Bible is relevant to the everyday person in society.

Dare I say that a refusal to engage society is unbiblical? In the sermons of Jesus, Peter, and Paul, we see a good emphasis on theology and yet also an understanding of their context (without the compromise of the message). One doesn't have to include a long diatribe when sharing hope with someone, but there should be knowledge of the customs of society. If the greatest commandment and deepest theology is to love God and love others (Matthew 22:37–40), then maybe our study of Scripture is part of "love God" and our study of culture is seen in "love others."

I remember when I got the iPhone 6. I was so stoked. There was a part of me that actually felt bad for those who had the iPhone 5. (I promise I'm not that much of a brat—it was just the excitement of having the latest technology.) Then something was released the following year: the iPhone 6s.

I thought, *Are you kidding me? Apple needs to calm down. I just caught up!* I didn't want everyone else to have the latest gadget, and I didn't want to feel as if I were tossed out in the cold again.

The feeling didn't last long and I went back to normal . . . until I went home one night. Then what to my wondering eyes did appear? My wife had an iPhone 6s. I couldn't believe it! She said, "Oh, I had to, Caleb. I dropped my phone in water." And she smiled at me.

If you're married, I don't know how you interpret your spouse's smile. Amy has different smiles, and each one communicates an emotion. I knew this particular smile. It was one of her favorite smiles. The smile she was beaming at me basically said, *I love you. I know it's going to drive you crazy that I have the latest Apple phone, and I'm okay with that because you entertain me when you get annoyed, kind of like a prank. But I really do love you.* Yes, one smile can say all that and more.

"Water?" I asked.

"Yes," she responded with the same smile. "Water."

Thoughts ran through my head, such as, *Well, it's convenient to have a puddle of water nearby.*

Now, more than ever, I felt like a toothless hillbilly living in the mountains by myself. I honestly had a moment when I tried to figure out how to ask my wife how we could work it out to where I could get the latest phone, but I refrained. For once, I refused to be a diva.

My point isn't to speak poorly of those who are two Apple phones behind, are cursed with a Samsung, or don't have any phone. My point is that we are always changing and moving. The biblical narrative never changes, but society is consistently shifting and moving.

Because society is always shifting, it's paramount to become students of society as much as we are students of theology. Why? Because we live in a time of polarizing beliefs, differing worldviews, obscure ideas, and competing systems.

Be Intentional in What You Say—It Can Take You a Long Way

Some Christians have great theological knowledge, along with an understanding of society, but fall short in crafting their message to be heard by others. I've heard some say the following: "Well, I'm not responsible for how my listeners interpret my words." That may be true to a degree, but sometimes I think those people who make such statements might be lazy. We can make it easier for those we are sharing the story of Jesus with to interpret our words correctly by being intentional in the words we use, the stories we tell, the Bible verses we share, the tone and body language we employ, and so on.

Throughout Acts 17:16–34, we see that Paul structured his message with his audience (academic scholars and philosophers) in mind. He called attention to their altar of the "unknown god" (verse 23) and surprised these philosophers by calling them "ignorant." I doubt Paul called them ignorant to offend them, but rather he knew they disdained ignorance, and they had already invited him to educate them (verses 19–20). If I had to guess, I bet this was the hook Paul knew would make them lean in and say, "Tell me more." At another point in his message, he quoted two of their poets and entertainers (verse 28), showing that he was current with their society.

Intentionality is all about knowing whom you are engaging and how to deliver the hope of Jesus in a way that a person can best hear. Being intentional in what we communicate doesn't mean we compromise the message. I'm sure there were further elements of theology Paul could have touched on in his message, but he didn't address them. His end goal was to get the Athenians to follow the true God (mission accomplished for some of them, according to verses 32–34). Paul was careful in what he said and what he didn't say. And that's a model for us.

We can be orthodox in our theology while committing heresy by how we treat others.

One way we can fail is to talk about a recent event in society in a way that offends people (even though we didn't mean to offend). A few years ago, I attended a conference in the South. It started on a Sunday night, so I flew there on Saturday and chose a church to attend on Sunday morning. There was a guest preacher that particular day. His sermon was pretty solid . . . until he got to the middle of his message. A certain celebrity I shall not name had just decided to divorce his wife, the news had hit the tabloids, and the celebrity had responded with some unwise words. That day the guest preacher decided to use the situation as an example of the consequences of not living a holy life. Not only did the guest preacher completely bash the celebrity, his spouse, and the rest of Hollywood but he also had no idea that family members of the celebrity attended this church—and they were in attendance on the day he was preaching. As you can imagine, the family took offense at how he described the celebrity.

Was the preacher right in what he said about holy living? I think so. Was the preacher wrong in how he handled it? Yes—100 percent wrong. Should he have even mentioned it? He could have mentioned it with more love and concern rather than use the celebrity as a tackling dummy for his sermon. Did the pastor present the celebrity and others in the story with compassion and as those whom God created and for whom Jesus died? Nope. His lack of intentionality showed that day, and it did damage to some good people. In other words, we can be orthodox in our theology while committing heresy by how we treat others.

Now, I know you're probably not a pastor like I am and like the poor misguided guest preacher who beat up, verbally, on the celebrity. But the same principle holds true for all followers of Jesus who are sharing their love of the Lord with friends and acquaintances who don't know him.

Am I saying we should never address people or the latest events? Not at all! Even Jesus and Paul addressed contemporary issues. I'm suggesting that we need to use intentionality in how we address specific situations or people. We can be gracious. We don't have to water down a call to truth, but we should realize that how we describe relevant events and people matters because the person we're relating with might have differing views.

As we think about how to be intentional with society, perhaps we could start with questions such as these:

- What kinds of words, names, and cultural references might offend others to the degree that they don't listen to much after that reference?
- When addressing an act or situation that I might see as sin and others might not, how can I still promote the truth with grace amid a tough subject?
- What are some recent stories of redemption in today's culture that I could use?

- Instead of talking *against* a sin the whole time (because people are so tied with their sin), how can I show that God is *for* people?

While these are good questions, it's not enough for us to be intentional. We have to go a step further.

Your Appeal Should Be Countercultural and, Well, Appealing

When we engage society, no matter how kind we are, we will be countercultural (because the gospel is countercultural). However, our attitude should never be *anti*cultural. If we're anticultural, we're unnecessarily combative in approach and usually offer no glimpse of grace, redemption, or God's present love for people. Remember, we don't have to fight or surrender to society, but we must engage society with bold conviction and graciousness. Both Paul and Jesus were countercultural to both the religious community and secular society. In a similar way, the church has always been countercultural, as has been the gospel. I love what my friend Carey Nieuwhof said:

> For most of the last 2000 years, the authentic church has been counter-cultural. The church was certainly counter-cultural in the first century.
>
> Even at the height of "Christendom" (whenever that was), the most conservative historians would agree that Christianity as embraced by the state was different than the authentic Christianity we read about in scripture or that was practiced by many devout followers of Jesus.
>
> Being counter-cultural usually helps the church more than hurts it.[1]

One of the many things I love about Jesus was how he was both countercultural and intriguing to those far from God. Paul was too. In Acts 17:19, Paul was taken to a meeting of the Areopagus after talking with these philosophers. In verse 32, the people listening to Paul wanted him to stay and keep lecturing. I doubt they would have done this if he had been rude or uncaring. For the Athenians, there was something appealing about Paul even though he was different from them. Obviously, his was the message of truth, but I believe that part of the appeal was his concern for them by understanding where they were. Again, this is nothing that Jesus didn't do during his earthly ministry.

As we engage society, we will have to deal more and more with difficult issues that will be lightning rods. While Jesus loved people, he was also so truthful at times that he caused some people to leave.

We can engage polarizing environments or people and still have maximum impact. Our knowledge of society helps us engage people to the point where their ears and hearts are primed for the gospel. The leaders in the New Testament understood this principle, and it was easy for people to see Jesus in their lives.

When I think of someone who understands this principle, Joseph Barkley comes to mind. After serving on staff at a church in the Los Angeles area, Joseph decided to step out in faith and start a church in the Hollywood area. You might ask, "Why start a church in Hollywood?" Because he wanted to go to a place where people really didn't go to church. While there are many good churches in the Hollywood area, there are few churches that are intentional about understanding that many unchurched people will never step foot inside a church unless a church is intentional about reaching them.

So, with faith and an understanding of the Hollywood context, Joseph started Radius Church. On their website they say they are "a church for people convinced church is irrelevant." They go on to say, "Radius is a place where you will be welcomed as you are. No judgement. No assumptions. No secret handshake."[2] Anyone attending Radius on a Sunday would find awesome worship, biblical and relevant teaching, and authentic people. Those attending find the layout and ministry environment different from most other churches because Radius knows the context of Hollywood and feels called to share God's hope in that setting.

Radius throws parties in the neighborhood from time to time to give people more exposure to their church. Joseph tells a funny story about a guy who approached him at one of these Radius parties. Not knowing that Joseph was the pastor, he walked over to Joseph during the party and said, "Did you know there are actually a lot of Christians here? And they're actually kind of normal."

Joseph responded to him, "I'm one of them."[3]

Then he leveraged that experience to tell him about Radius and invite him to a service. The next Sunday, the guy showed up at Radius. While this is a funny story, it also shows the intentionality Radius has for understanding their context for sharing Jesus.

When people look at your life, it should be so easy for them to see Jesus in how you treat them, love them, and share truth with them.

And how has Radius done? It's actually grown tremendously! Not only have they been successful in reaching people who otherwise didn't attend church, but many people also attend who have been Christians for a while and wanted to partner with a church to reach their unchurched community.

What about you? While God might not be calling you to start a church, where is he calling you to take a step of faith and enter into your context with intentionality? As you grow in your God-inspired confidence, which of the people in your circle will you try to share Jesus with? Maybe you haven't been so successful with this in the past. How can you do it differently? What changes need to take place in your heart as well as in your strategy?

In a society that has become as diverse and fast changing as ours, learning to communicate across divides is becoming a necessary and ongoing task. It's hard work, for sure. But the alternative is that real communication will cease and that if people even get a chance to hear the gospel, their reaction will be *Huh?*

When people look at your life, it should be so easy for them to see Jesus in how you treat them, love them, and share truth with them. Individuals should be able to look at you and say, "There's something different about you." Getting to this point is extremely hard, but it is absolutely necessary in our day and age.

Our lives, our engagement and investment in others, our posture toward people, and our words should make it easy for people to see Jesus in us and the tomorrow he offers. Are you with me?

REFLECTION AND DISCUSSION QUESTIONS

1. In Acts 17:16–34, Paul was very strategic in how he related to the Athenian philosophers. In what ways was he strategic in his approach?

2. Why is it important for us to study not only the Bible but also our current society? How can we become good students of society?

3. How does the intentionality of our words and actions make it easier for people to hear Jesus's message?

4. Do you believe it's possible for our message to be true and countercultural while at the same time being appealing? Why or why not? Is one more important than the other?

5. As you consider the times you've shared the gospel, have your words, actions, and character made it easy for people to see Jesus in you? How can you improve in one or more of these areas? Before you move on to the next chapter, begin to brainstorm a plan for improving the way you tell others about Jesus.

TOMORROW BELONGS TO GOD, NOT YOU.

12

The God of Tomorrow . . . and Today

Sweat dripped into his eyes, stinging them, and he couldn't wipe it away. He was nailed to two pieces of wood that formed a cross. His body was stressed beyond belief. When he pulled his body up by the nails in his hands, he could breathe, but it increased the pain. As he reached the point of excruciating pain, he'd let go and slump back down on the cross. Now he couldn't breathe. This continuous juggling of pain and need to breathe was bad, but his thoughts were drawn to the impending death that awaited him. He feared what awaited him after he departed this world.

He wasn't the only one being crucified that day. There were two other men. One of them was another man who had broken the law. It might even be a good guess that the first criminal personally knew the other lawbreaker, the second criminal, who was setting the record straight with the sacrifice of his life.

The third man being crucified that day was in between the two criminals and wasn't like them. As a matter of fact, I bet since the first criminal knew what being a bad guy was all about, he could immediately tell that this "Jesus of Nazareth, King of the Jews" was unlike any person he'd ever heard of who had received the death penalty.

What was even more peculiar was how Jesus was being treated in his remaining hours on earth. The citizens and religious leaders yelled things such as, "He saved others; let him save himself if he is God's Messiah, the Chosen One" (Luke 23:35). If that wasn't enough, the Roman soldiers chimed in with their own mockery: "If you are the king of the Jews, save yourself" (verse 37). It almost seemed as if the death of this one man was unifying everyone at the foot of his cross. Those you would never expect to agree on anything—Roman soldiers, Jewish religious leaders, and ordinary citizens—suddenly agreed with one another that this teacher deserved death.

In the beginning, the first criminal joined in the insults, but soon he had a change of heart. Perhaps he stopped because he realized how hypocritical he was. But the second criminal wasn't stopping his verbal jabs. He was using his last breaths to curse and make fun of this innocent rabbi. How audacious!

Taking all this in, the first criminal probably knew he didn't have enough moral authority to rebuke the crowds, but he could rebuke this other criminal. Looking in the direction of the other criminal, he took a stand for an innocent man. "Don't you fear God," he said, "since you are under the same sentence? We are punished justly, for we are getting what our deeds deserve. But this man has done nothing wrong" (verses 40–41).

According to the words of the first criminal, the second criminal who harassed Jesus made three mistakes. As one Bible scholar put it, "(1) Rather than fearing God, he maligns God's instrument of salvation. (2) He assumes that Jesus is guilty when, in fact, he is innocent. (3) In his sarcasm, he fails to recognize that this Suffering Righteous One will be delivered not from but through death, and that he will continue to exercise his role as Savior."[1] How did the first criminal come to these conclusions? My question is, if he was really observing Jesus, how could he *not* come to these conclusions?

It would be reasonable to assume that this criminal had seen men cry in the face of death or scream at others in the face of death, but he had never seen a man act like Jesus in the face of death. The criminal could tell that Jesus not only was being verbally attacked by everyone around him but had already been beaten, severely flogged, and worn out from carrying the crossbeam down the street. Yet despite all Jesus had been through, he still had the strength to look death straight in the eye and not blink. He had the humility to not respond to evil. It could be that Jesus was looking beyond that day and into *tomorrow*.

I believe seeing Jesus die with such strength helped this criminal take a bold step in faith that he never thought he would take. "Jesus, remember me when you come into your kingdom," the criminal humbly asked (verse 42).

What a statement! I believe that this criminal might be the most faithful person in the Bible. In that moment, he might have been one of the only people on the face of the earth who really believed that Jesus was the Messiah. No doubt the people who heard the criminal's request turned their harsh words toward him. I mean, who would ever believe that this homeless ex-carpenter rabbi was really a king? Perhaps the people below the cross thought that if he was, it was a very weak and poor kingdom.

The first criminal was about to experience the best this day had to offer . . .

THE PARADISE PROMISE

Jesus raised his head, looked at the criminal, and said to him, "Truly I tell you, today you will be with me in paradise" (verse 43). Even in Jesus's dying moments, he was concerned about those near him and was willing to forgive them. Jesus used what little breath he could muster to assure the first criminal of his place in God's presence. What words to hear from Jesus! I seriously believe that in this moment, the words of Jesus gave the repentant criminal the strength to push through the most painful moments of his slow death. The promise of *paradise today* holds a lot of weight.

The word translated *paradise* means "garden" or "the dwelling of the righteous."[2] Paul used this word in 2 Corinthians 12:4 when he talked about his own brief trip to heaven. Jesus used this same word in Revelation 2:7: "To the one who is victorious, I will give the right to eat from the tree of life, which is in the paradise of God." So, this unrighteous criminal who admitted that he deserved death was now promised a place with those God considered righteous—those having no fault, no guilty verdict, no accusatory words thrown at them.

Jesus said this first criminal would be in paradise with righteous people *today*. Contrary to the beliefs of some first-century experts, he wouldn't have to go to Sheol (the place of the dead) first, nor would he have to linger as a spirit for a couple of days or more. No, *today* was the day when he would experience paradise.

And don't misunderstand why he would experience paradise today. It wasn't because he was a good person or performed a charitable act. The first criminal wasn't a good person, and he was completely powerless, at the weakest point of his life. His place in paradise was assured by a single sentence from the King of kings. The same one who spoke all things into existence (Colossians 1:16–17) was speaking the criminal's righteousness into today and tomorrow. One day when we are all in paradise, it will be fascinating to understand these events from the perspective of the criminal himself. That will be quite the story to hear.

THE GOD WHO IS WITH YOU

The paradise Jesus offers is for *all* those who follow Jesus. You and I have the same promise today that the first criminal did. God tells us that when we follow Jesus, we, too, will one day be with him in paradise. Exodus 34:6 reminds us, "The LORD, the LORD, the compassionate and gracious God, slow to anger, abounding in love and faithfulness." God is gracious when we don't expect him to be. He's slow to anger when we would be quick to get even or impulsively right a wrong. God doesn't just show love—he *abounds* in love for the world. He is completely committed and faithful to those he loves.

God doesn't just show love—he *abounds* in love for the world.

God will never leave or abandon you. He's with you no matter what happens in society, and he has always been with you! In Matthew 1:23, the angel Gabriel told Joseph that Jesus's name, Immanuel, means "God with us." At the end of the same book in 28:20, Jesus promised his followers, "I am with you always, to the very end of the age."

In the first three chapters of the Bible's first book, Genesis, we see that God was among humanity in a way he is not today. But in the last three chapters of the Bible, Revelation 20–22, we discover that in the future, God will be among his people again in a very special way. In other words, the beginning and end of Matthew promise us that God came to be with us and that he is always with us.

God was working in your life before you were ever born. He is present and active in our world, even when you don't see it. The worst thing could happen to you, and God would still be in your corner. My favorite chapter of the Bible contains a verse that I've found myself clinging to during some of my darkest days: "We know that in all things God works for the good of those who love him, who have been called according to his purpose" (Romans 8:28).

The moment you're in a relationship with God, even if you go in a wrong direction, he is still there. Paul reminds us,

> If we are faithless,
> he remains faithful,
> for he cannot disown himself. (2 Timothy 2:13)

He's so faithful that he's eager to forgive our wrongdoings. We see this fact mentioned by the apostle John: "If we confess our sins, he is faithful and just and will forgive us our sins and purify us from all un-righteousness" (1 John 1:9). God is just like the father in the parable of the prodigal son who hugged his son even before the young man could finish his rehearsed apology speech (Luke 15:20).

When our expectations of God don't align with the reality of what happens in life, he is still with us.

As times get tough in life, God is still there. When we feel beat up by the words of others, God is there. Just because the trends of society seem to move away from God's values, he doesn't move away from us. God isn't going anywhere.

When war appears unending, God will one day give us peace and justice.

When tragedy takes lives unexpectedly, God leads us to comfort the hurting.

When Christians are bullied for their values, God will be their defense.

When families split apart, God offers a family that will never divide.

When the abused are too fearful to stand, God sends us to lift them up.

When children are left as orphans, God chooses us to adopt as he adopted us.

When injustice seems to increase, God is poised and ready to return with justice.

When society undergoes changes, God will remain unchanging.

Whatever we're facing today doesn't reflect God's promises for us tomorrow. He won't change his mind about us or about being with us. Our current circumstances aren't a reflection of how he feels about us. When our expectations of God don't align with the reality of what happens in life, he is still with us. He hasn't left us. Sometime soon the next big lightning-rod issue or horrible event will arrive in society, and God will be present just as he always has been. Our hope transcends what is today and trusts in what God will do tomorrow.

BACK TO THE STREETS OF CINCINNATI

Remember in the beginning of the book when I talked about the culture clash I saw in the streets of Cincinnati on June 26, 2015? Recall my acquaintance in the convention center who was exiting the main session? Perhaps you remember his words that bothered me:

"I don't know what tomorrow holds."

Well, he was right. He didn't know, and I didn't know. I'm not all knowing, all powerful, unchanging, eternal, or any other attribute of God you want to throw in there. Neither are you. None of us has a clue what tomorrow holds. *But through Christ we know the one who holds tomorrow.* We know the God of tomorrow . . . and today.

I walked out of the convention center after talking with a few friends and noticed that what once had been a cloudy day was beginning to reveal some sun. But the actual sunlight wasn't the only thing that brightened my day. Standing outside the convention center, I saw some of the Christian leaders who had been in attendance that week interacting with those celebrating on sidewalks. I noticed a leader talking with a man who seemed homeless. Other pastors who were leaving the convention center started praying outside because of the Supreme Court decision on marriage equality. I didn't see anyone from the LGBTQ community screaming at them for doing so, nor did I notice any Christian leaders yelling at those who disagreed with their prayers. The hope in my heart started to rise because I saw few Christians (if any) walk indifferently past those who were difficult for them.

In that moment God reminded me that *hope is always available.* I began right then to glimpse the principle we have examined, tested, and applied in this book.

The God of Tomorrow Principle

Since tomorrow belongs to God, we can graciously offer hope to people today.

It's a beautiful truth, isn't it? All followers of Jesus are free to continue to invest in society with hope for tomorrow. Our hope is authenticated by God's plan that is certain to be fulfilled.

WHAT MUST HAPPEN

A few years ago, a friend of mine who was a seminary professor challenged me to do a study on the word *must* in the book of Revelation. I found that this word is used seven times in the book. Let me start with the first six instances, and see if you notice their commonality.

1. "The revelation from Jesus Christ, which God gave him to show his servants what *must* soon take place" (1:1).

2. "After this I looked, and there before me was a door standing open in heaven. And the voice I had first heard speaking to me like a trumpet said, 'Come up here, and I will show you what *must* take place after this'" (4:1).

3. "If anyone tries to harm them, fire comes from their mouths and devours their enemies. This is how anyone who wants to harm them *must* die" (11:5).

4. "They are also seven kings. Five have fallen, one is, the other has not yet come; but when he does come, he *must* remain for only a little while" (17:10).

5. "He threw him into the Abyss, and locked and sealed it over him, to keep him from deceiving the nations anymore until the thousand years were ended. After that, he *must* be set free for a short time" (20:3).

6. "The angel said to me, 'These words are trustworthy and true. The Lord, the God who inspires the prophets, sent his angel to show his servants the things that *must* soon take place'" (22:6).

Each of the first six *must*s in Revelation highlights what will certainly happen in the plan of God. The seventh *must* is different. It refers not only to the plan of God but also to the fact that we are to do something in accordance with his plan.

7. "I was told, 'You *must* prophesy again about many peoples, nations, languages and kings'" (10:11).

What God says "must" happen in his plan will take people on a journey to tomorrow. God says we need to invest in society—whatever society we're in and the global culture around us. Our conviction to engage today will be defined by our view of God's control of tomorrow. If we hold a high view of God, we will be confident in our engagement of tomorrow. Will we face obstacles, opposition, and evil? Yes, of course. But God has already taken care of things. Evil has been defeated, though not yet destroyed.

Through the cross of Christ, evil has been overcome, but it is something we still have to face in our society. Our strength to face today comes from the hope that God offers tomorrow. We cannot forget this truth, or else tomorrow will seem even vaguer. I love what my friend Troy Fountain said: "We get so focused on the urgent and temporal that we lose sight of the important and eternal."[3]

So true.

God has already been to the tomorrow you're excited about.

God has already seen the tomorrow you're dreading.

Tomorrow belongs to God, not you.

If God has seen the future, then his power will take you there, because tomorrow belongs to him. He has been there, is fully present there, created it, prepared it, planned it, fashioned it, and will walk with us from today into tomorrow—no matter what tomorrow has in store.

Tomorrow belongs to God, not you.

If we believe that God prepared tomorrow and will walk with us into it, then we can have the courage to make a difference today.

Everything New

Early on in my ministry, I used to love to perform weddings. Today? Not so much. Don't get me wrong—I'll do a wedding here and there for someone I know really well. But it now takes a lot for me to agree to perform one.

There are just so many things about weddings that drain me. No matter when they're scheduled, it eats up the day. Some wedding coordinators are not the easiest people to communicate with. Members of the wedding party sometimes forget to bend their knees and end up passing out (in one wedding I performed, one groomsman and one bridesmaid fainted). You must wait around and make small talk with people you don't know (although the invention of the iPhone has created a great distraction). Hunting down the happy couple for the wedding license, obtaining witness signatures, and reminding someone about the honorarium is never fun. A lot of the rehearsals I've participated in seem to include tension between the bride and one of the moms of the couple. The worst case is if the wedding is outdoors in the summer without shade and the sun beats down on your bald head. (Okay, so maybe that one is just me.)

One particular wedding took me to Camarillo, California, where I was standing in front of a huge white mansion. It was nestled in the middle of town, and it was one of the most beautiful places I have ever been to. The house was adjacent to a huge gravel parking lot and was surrounded by trees of all kinds, but mostly palm trees. Looking around the property, I was surprised by how large it was. There were a couple of smaller houses, two gazebos, bright-green grass amid a drought, and apparently every kind of plant known to humanity.

Even though it was late afternoon in August and the sun was still out, the trees provided shade. But it was still hot! I began to sweat under my T-shirt, dress shirt, and suit coat. I took off my sunglasses and peered into the house. Absolutely no one was there yet. Slowly, though, people started arriving. The wedding actually started on time, and I was eager to finish the ceremony.

There's one part of the wedding that I always think is beautiful: the bride.

I remember looking at my Amy as she walked down the aisle on our wedding day. I'll admit it—I cried. As she walked down the aisle, she seemed radiant, not only because of the magnificent dress she was wearing but also from the radiant smile she brought with her. In that moment, all I heard was this word echoing in my head: *beautiful, beautiful, beautiful . . .*

I'll never forget that day.

As the bride walked down the path to her groom on this beautiful sunny day in Camarillo, I couldn't help but think that all the work, money, sacrifice, tears, and more were worth it. In that moment, absolutely no one could steal the bride and groom's joy.

In the same way, one of the tomorrows that comes our way will carry with it Christ's return. The church will be presented to Christ as a bride is presented to her groom. When Christ returns, we will be with him for eternity.

God promises in Revelation 21:3–5 that our tomorrow will one day hold this comfort:

> "God's dwelling place is now among the people, and he will dwell with them. They will be his people, and God himself will be with them and be their God. 'He will wipe every tear from their eyes. There will be no more death' or mourning or crying or pain, for the old order of things has passed away."
>
> He who was seated on the throne said, "I am making everything new!"

Tomorrow has *everything new.*

With bold voices and gracious postures at our disposal, let's invest in and offer people the hope of God's tomorrow. Through God's power, we can be instruments to change society and transform the world, one relationship at a time.

And leave the fear behind because you know the God of Tomorrow.

REFLECTION AND DISCUSSION QUESTIONS

1. How did the criminal on the cross show his faith in Jesus's power over tomorrow?

2. Read Romans 8:1, 28–31 and 2 Timothy 2:13. What do these verses have to say about Jesus's followers?

3. God is with you no matter what you do or what happens in society. How have you seen this to be true in your life?

4. Reread the seven "must" verses in Revelation. What do these verses tell you about God's power and plan?

5. God's power and plan will lead all of us to a place that is described in Revelation 21:3–5. There is nothing to fear because God has created, purposed, and been to tomorrow, and he will journey with us there. As you finish this book, pray for him to strip you of any of your toxic fears regarding people and replace them with incredible faith that comes from knowing the God of Tomorrow.

Acknowledgments

Amy, I'm so glad to be on this journey called life with you. More than most, you've taught me many of the principles in this book by how you've loved me. I love you.

Joel and Rachel, you are growing into the beautiful, bold, and gracious people I have always prayed for you to be. Keep looking to Jesus! I love you both.

Don Gates, as always, you aren't just my agent, but you're also my good friend and ministry partner. You empower so many of us to change the lives of others. Thank you.

Susan Tjaden, you've been a cheerleader and supporter of the ideas behind this book for some time now. You are an amazing friend, editor, leader, and visionary. It's truly an honor to work with you.

Eric Stanford, your commitment to excellence and patience with me made this project so valuable. You made it happen. I appreciate you and am proud to call you a friend.

Carey Nieuwhof, over these past few years you've truly become a good friend. Thank you for listening, laughing, praying, and even just being fully present in our conversations. I'm so glad to have someone like you in my life. You make me better.

Lane Jones, thank you for being the voice of reason and holding me accountable to living out these principles in my own life, even when I don't want to! I'm glad to call you a friend. Also, Disneyland is way better than Disney World.

Ashley Wooldridge, in our many conversations, you've always

reminded me that humility trumps pride—God blesses humility but never pride. I'm grateful for your friendship and voice in my life.

Joseph Barkley, your ministry is making a difference in the lives of people in ways you don't know. If you weren't there, they wouldn't have a church like yours. Never give up.

Barry Corey, I'm glad you're the president of my alma mater. More than most I know, you are an embodiment of grace and kindness. Please keep setting that example.

Stan Jantz, the interest you've taken in me has turned into a relationship that has been an encouragement. I'm grateful for you.

Troy Fountain, there are few people who can make me laugh and convict me in the same conversation. You do both well. Love you, bro.

To the guys on my call groups—Matt Braun, Jeff Brodie, James Brummett, Rusty George, Al Scott, Sean Seay, and Ben Snyder—our calls challenge me to lead well. Thank you for speaking into my life, looking past my flaws, and accepting me, even when I joined one of our Skype calls after just getting out of the shower!

Notes

Chapter 1: Punched by Tomorrow

1. William Shakespeare, *Macbeth,* 5.5.19–21.

Chapter 2: God Isn't Afraid

1. *Fantastic Beasts and Where to Find Them,* directed by David Yates (London: Heyday Films; Burbank, CA: Warner Bros., 2016), www.imdb.com/title/tt3183660/quotes.
2. J. Dwight Pentecost, *Thy Kingdom Come: Tracing God's Kingdom Program and Covenant Promises Throughout History* (Grand Rapids, MI: Kregel, 1995), 28.
3. Faith Karimi, Catherine E. Shoichet, and Ralph Ellis, "Dallas Sniper Attack: 5 Officers Killed, Suspect Identified," *CNN,* July 9, 2016, www.cnn.com/2016/07/08/us/philando-castile-alton-sterling-protests/.

Chapter 3: Leverage the Relationship

1. Martin Heidegger, *Being and Time,* trans. Joan Stambaugh (Albany, NY: SUNY Press, 2010), 33.
2. *Creed,* directed by Ryan Coogler (Beverly Hills, CA: Metro-Goldwyn-Mayer, 2015); "Creed—I'm Ready Scene (4/11)," YouTube video, 3:29, posted by Movieclips, December 14, 2016, www.youtube.com/watch?v=jyNtMzHeJ6I.
3. "Only a God Can Save Us," trans. Maria P. Alter and John D. Caputo, interview with Der Spiegel, *Philosophy Today* 20 (April 4, 1976): 267–85.

4. David Blair, "The World Has over 45 Million Slaves—Including 1.2 Million in Europe—Finds New Study," *The Telegraph,* May 31, 2016, www.telegraph.co.uk/news/2016/05/31/the-world-has -over-45-million-slaves---including-12-million-in-e/.

5. Seana Scott, "How a Disney Ballerina Ended Up Fighting Modern Slavery," *Christianity Today,* April 2017, www.christianitytoday .com/women/2017/april/how-disney-ballerina-ended-up-fighting -modern-slavery.html.

Chapter 4: Society Is Like an Emergency Room on New Year's Eve

1. "Fear Leads to Anger, Anger Leads to Hate, Hate . . . to Suffering," July 15, 2010, posted by Gabriel Wennberg, YouTube video, :08, www.youtube.com/watch?v=kFnFr-DOPf8.

Chapter 5: Developing a Love-Thy-Neighbor Attitude

1. *Wikipedia,* s.v. "RMS *Titanic,*" https://en.wikipedia.org/wiki /RMS_Titanic#Sinking.

2. From a personal conversation with the author.

3. William Gurnall, *The Christian in Complete Armour: A Treatise of the Saints' War Against the Devil,* vol. 2 (London: Blackie and Son, 1865), 568.

4. Dietrich Bonhoeffer, *Letters and Papers from Prison* (New York: Touchstone, 1997), 382.

Chapter 6: For Relationship, Start Here

1. Quoted in Jim Korkis, "When Roy E. Disney Resigned from Disney Twice," *Mouse Planet,* April 13, 2016, www.mouseplanet .com/11377/When_Roy_E_Disney_Resigned_from_Disney _Twice.

2. Brené Brown, "Brené Brown on Empathy vs Simpathy [*sic*]," YouTube video, 2:53, posted by Diana Simon Psihoterapeut, April 1, 2016, www.youtube.com/watch?v=KZBTYViDPlQ.

3. Quoted in Regi Campbell, "Radical Empathy and the Second Question," *Radical Mentoring* (blog), October 24, 2016, https://radicalmentoring.com/radical-empathy-second-question/?utm _content=buffer02e01&utm_medium=social&utm_source =twitter.com&utm_campaign=buffer.

4. Reggie Joiner, evening session at the Orange Conference, April 26, 2017, Duluth, Georgia.

5. Louie Giglio and Matt Redman, *Indescribable: Encountering the Glory of God in the Beauty of the Universe* (Colorado Springs, CO: David C Cook, 2011), 159.

Chapter 7: Impersonating the Oppressed

1. "Statistics," Bound4Life, www. bound4life.com/statistics/.

2. Leonor Vivanco and Dawn Rhodes, "U. of C. Tells Incoming Freshmen It Does Not Support 'Trigger Warnings' or 'Safe Spaces,'" *Chicago Tribune,* August 25, 2016, www.chicagotribune.com/news /local/breaking/ct-university-of-chicago-safe-spaces-letter-met-20160 825-story.html. A trigger warning is a statement at the beginning of a presentation that it contains material that may be distressing to some.

3. *The Hobbit: An Unexpected Journey,* directed by Peter Jackson (Burbank, CA: Warner Bros., 2012), www.imdb.com/title/tt09036 24/quotes. The quotation is not in J. R. R. Tolkien's original book.

Chapter 8: The Injustice of Indifference

1. Andy Wong, "Dennis Rodman: North Korea Isn't So Bad," *CBS News,* January 5, 2014, www.cbsnews.com/news/dennis-rodman -north-korea-isnt-so-bad/.

2. Ella Wheeler Wilcox, "Protest," in *Poems of Problems* (Chicago: W. B. Conkey, 1914), 154.
3. Dwight D. Eisenhower, inaugural address, January 20, 1953, www.presidency.ucsb.edu/ws/?pid=9600.
4. Priscilla Alvarez, "When Sex Trafficking Goes Unnoticed in America: Many Cases Go Unreported, Making It a Difficult Crime for Law Enforcement Personnel to Spot," *The Atlantic,* February 23, 2016, www.theatlantic.com/politics/archive/2016 /02/how-sex-trafficking-goes-unnoticed-in-america/470166/.

Chapter 9: Making Tomorrow Great Again

1. Stephen R. Miller, *The New American Commentary: Daniel,* vol. 18 (Nashville: Broadman & Holman, 1994), 93.
2. Miller, *New American Commentary,* 95.
3. Miller, *New American Commentary,* 95.

Chapter 10: No More Christian Bullies

1. " 'Stop It' Skit by Bob Newhart," Vimeo video, 6:21, posted by Tim Tolosa, June 4, 2014, https://vimeo.com/97370236.
2. David Kinnaman and Gabe Lyons, *unChristian: What a New Generation Really Thinks About Christianity . . . and Why It Matters* (Grand Rapids, MI: Baker, 2007), 52.
3. Charles Spurgeon, *All of Grace: Know That God's Gift of Salvation Is Absolutely Free and Available to Everyone* (Uhrichsville, OH: Barbour, 2014), 24.

Chapter 11: Bullhorns Aren't Loud Enough

1. Carey Nieuwhof, "Some Advice on Same-Sex Marriage for US Church Leaders from a Canadian," *Carey Nieuwhof* (blog),

June 29, 2015, http://careynieuwhof.com/some-advice-on-same
-sex-marriage-for-us-church-leaders-from-a-canadian/.

2. "Welcome to Radius," Radius Church, www.radius.la/#welcome
-to-radius-1-2.

3. Rachael Lee, "Los Angeles Churches Unite to Plant 'a Gospel-
Driven Church for Every Neighborhood,'" *Christianity Daily,*
October 9, 2015, www.christianitydaily.com/articles/6392
/20151009/los-angeles-churches-unite-plant-gospel-driven
-church-neighborhood.htm.

Chapter 12: The God of Tomorrow . . . and Today

1. Joel B. Green, *The New International Commentary on the New
Testament: The Gospel of Luke* (Grand Rapids, MI: Eerdmans,
1997), 822.

2. Darrell L. Bock, *Luke: 9:51–24:53, Baker Exegetical Commentary
on the New Testament* (Grand Rapids, MI: Baker, 1996): 2:1857.

3. From a personal conversation with the author.

Reading List

Out of the many books that tackle the subject of how society and faith intersect, the following are some I would recommend. While you and I may have different perspectives than some of these authors, each has valuable insights for consideration.

Barna, George, and David Kinnaman, eds. *Churchless: Understanding Today's Unchurched and How to Connect with Them.* Carol Stream, IL: Tyndale Momentum, 2014.

Bock, Darrell L. *How Would Jesus Vote? Do Your Political Views Really Align with the Bible?* Brentwood, TN: Howard, 2016.

Corey, Barry H. *Love Kindness: Discover the Power of a Forgotten Christian Virtue.* Carol Stream, IL: Tyndale, 2016.

Daly, Jim, with Paul Batura. *ReFocus: Living a Life That Reflects God's Heart.* Grand Rapids, MI: Zondervan, 2012.

Foster, Mike. *People of the Second Chance: A Guide to Bringing Life-Saving Love to the World.* Colorado Springs, CO: WaterBrook, 2016.

Hambrick, John. *Move Toward the Mess: The Ultimate Fix for a Boring Christian Life.* Colorado Springs, CO: David C Cook, 2016.

Harlow, Tim. *Life on Mission: God's People Finding God's Heart for the World.* Pastors.com, 2014.

Joiner, Reggie. *Zombies, Football and the Gospel: At Least 10 Somewhat Irrefutable Game-Changers for Church Leaders and Whoever They Follow.* Cumming, GA: reThink Group, 2012.

Keller, Timothy. *Making Sense of God: An Invitation to the Skeptical.* New York: Viking, 2016.

Loritts, Bryan, ed. *Letters to a Birmingham Jail: A Response to the Words and Dreams of Dr. Martin Luther King Jr.* Chicago: Moody, 2014.

Moore, Russell. *Onward: Engaging the Culture Without Losing the Gospel.* Nashville: B&H, 2015.

Powell, Kara, Jake Mulder, and Brad Griffin. *Growing Young: Six Essential Strategies to Help Young People Discover and Love Your Church.* Grand Rapids, MI: Baker, 2016.

Rae, Scott B. *Doing the Right Thing: Making Moral Choices in a World Full of Options.* Grand Rapids, MI: Zondervan, 2013.

Sauls, Scott. *Befriend: Create Belonging in an Age of Judgment, Isolation, and Fear.* Carol Stream, IL: Tyndale, 2016.

Stetzer, Ed. *Subversive Kingdom: Living as Agents of Gospel Transformation.* Nashville: B&H, 2012.

Volf, Miroslav, and Ryan McAnnally-Linz. *Public Faith in Action: How to Think Carefully, Engage Wisely, and Vote with Integrity.* Grand Rapids, MI: Brazos, 2016.

Weece, Jon. *Jesus Prom: Life Gets Fun When You Love People Like God Does.* Nashville: Thomas Nelson, 2014.

Wilson, Jared C. *Unparalleled: How Christianity's Uniqueness Makes It Compelling.* Grand Rapids, MI: Baker, 2016.

SOMETIMES, GRACE GETS MESSY.

Messy Grace shows us that Jesus's command to "love your neighbor as yourself" doesn't have an exception clause for a gay "neighbor" —or any other "neighbor" we might find it hard to relate to. Jesus loved everyone without compromising truth. So can we. Even when it's messy.

Learn more about Caleb's books at WaterBrookMultnomah.com.